Modern Hebrew Literature

Modern Hebrew Literature

From the Enlightenment
to the Birth of the State of Israel:
Trends and Values

SIMON HALKIN

SCHOCKEN BOOKS • NEW YORK

FOR Minnie, Zefira, and Hillel

CONTENTS

SINCE ITS first appearance in 1950, *Modern Hebrew Literature* has been acknowledged as an indispensable guide to this crucial period in the development of modern Judaism. The book opens with the Jewish Enlightenment in the first half of the eighteenth century and concludes appropriately with the foundation of the State of Israel. It is hoped that in its new edition this recently unavailable work will be able to serve an even wider audience. To that end, the biographical sketches in the "Guide to Authors" section have been updated where necessary. Otherwise, the publisher thought best to reissue the work without change.

The author—poet, novelist, literary historian, and critic—who for many years taught in the United States, is professor emeritus of Hebrew Literature at the Hebrew University, Jerusalem.

THIS WORK is not intended to be a history of modern Hebrew literature. While the material it investigates is exclusively literary, it is primarily a study of the socio-historical forces which have motivated Jewish life during the last two centuries. I have traced the development of modern Hebrew literature as a mirror reflecting those forces, and no other instrument could have suited my purposes more perfectly. I regard modern Hebrew literature as the most faithful and comprehensive record of Jewish life during this period. The major trends and values discernible in its evolution are the intimate, often passionate expression of the tangled problems which have haunted Jewry in this epoch.

The era since 1750 has been most remarkable in terms of human progress and human destructiveness. Likewise for the Jewish people the past two centuries are a record of unparalleled destruction and unparalleled creativity. On the one hand the historic mold of Jewish life in the Diaspora was continuously decomposing under the combined onslaught of assimilation, or spiritual disintegration, within, and physical suffering, ultimately physical extermination, without; on the other hand, the Jewish people was concentrating all the physical and spiritual forces it could yet muster for survival in its far-flung defenseless dispersion, and for the last-ditch stand it so heroically made on the soil of its historic homeland, now the State of Israel. The importance of analyzing the social and historical forces that have operated during this period is self-evident, for they are still very much with us, constantly engaging the attention of the Jewish historian from whatever angle he approaches them. Modern Hebrew literature—aside from purely aesthetic considerations—has been affected by these factors more consciously and articulated them more dramatically than any other contemporary literature; with the possible exception of the Russian. For that reason alone, perhaps, the study of modern Hebrew literature constitutes a unique problem of literary research.

This is the first attempt in any language to treat the whole history of modern Hebrew literature ideologically rather than from the standpoint of purely literary appreciation. Naturally, therefore, while I have followed the chronological sequence of events in the growth of this literature, I have not concerned myself chiefly with the critical evaluation of individual Hebrew authors; but rather with delineating the universe of thought in which they moved. This is also the first attempt to treat organically the development of current Hebrew literature in Israel. The reader may note that the material in this book is almost evenly divided between the last fifty years and the earlier one hundred and fifty. Chronologically, all decades are of equal length; historically, the events of a given brief span may be of such decisive importance as to overshadow those of longer periods. Such historical events must necessarily become the focal points of historical research, while the years preceding them may be viewed as gestatory.

The tremendous upheavals in the history of East European Jewry in the last fifty years, the destruction of Jewry in recent years, and the emergence of the State of Israel in

1948, are the overwhelming events in the past twenty centuries of Jewish history. In their light, all Jewish historiography will have to refocus its perspective. Hebrew literature has been aware of the historical significance of these decades. It has recorded their throes almost seismographically. Quantitatively and qualitatively, as if to keep pace with the rush of the events that have nurtured it, it has expanded out of all proportion to whatever development it had in the previous hundred and fifty years.

It is indeed unfortunate that a literature so dramatically social should have been so deplorably neglected by both the general reader and the student of Jewish life and history. Even more regrettable, perhaps, the literature produced in Israel in the past thirty years, the only authentic record of the inner forces that created the Jewish state, is equally little known. It is to be hoped that this book will in some measure fill the gap, paving the way for acquaintance with a humanly rich body of letters, and opening up a more correct perspective of modern Jewish history.

I should like here to tender my warm thanks to several friends for all they have done to enable me to prepare this book for publication prior to my departure for Israel. Nahum N. Glatzer, who carefully read the early draft of the book, suggested the plan for its revision; Miss Clara G. Stillman assisted with the preparation of the manuscript and I owe her an inexpressible debt; Milton Arfa constructed the Guide. To my wife, Minnie, to whom this book is dedicated, I am profoundly indebted: had it not been for her constant urging and encouragement, the book might not have emerged in its present form.

S. HALKIN

CHAPTER I

The Quest for a
New Life

MODERN Hebrew literature is the product of the last two hundred years of Jewish life; and two hundred years are a relatively brief span in a history that encompasses three thousand years of growth and development, of inner and outer struggle. Yet, the changes produced in Jewish life the world over by the revolutionary trends of this period have proved so overwhelming that modern Hebrew writing, which has striven to comprehend those changes, to interpret them, if not to determine their directions and ultimate goals, has resulted in a body of letters that is quantitatively richer and qualitatively more complex than is generally known.

During many centuries the Jewish tradition, while at times absorbing certain alien cultural influences—Hellenistic, Islamic, occidental—remained fundamentally exclusive. Self-sufficiency was the keynote. However much they took over from other sources, or contributed to them, the Jews always felt themselves justified in their self-segregation from the rest of the world.

But two hundred years ago this self-sufficiency began to be shaken. With the advent of the modern world Jewish life began to undergo a series of vicissitudes, unprecedented in all its history. It came out of its seclusion and began to reach out for Western culture, extending, broadening, and complicating its own vision and its relations with the modern world, sometimes gradually, sometimes with an almost shattering impact to its own deepest essence. In seeking to possess itself of the fruits of modern thought and experience, and fit itself into the new social-economic life which the French Revolution and the period of industrialization had initiated, it enlarged its horizon and increased its possibilities of development and influence; but it also found itself faced with a complex of new and disturbing problems, while many of its old tensions intensified in new forms.

During these two hundred years the Jewish people has striven to break away from the traditional patterns of its self-contained existence, to normalize and humanize its life materially and spiritually, to achieve greater happiness in all aspects of worldly existence: political and economic, social and cultural. And one of the most remarkable phenomena of this revolutionary change was the Hebrew literature that sprang into being with it, kept pace with it and reflected faithfully its innumerable facets, its strivings, victories and defeats, its sorrows and rejoicings. In poetry and prose, modern Hebrew literature has interpreted and evaluated the historic drama of the emergence of the modern Jew from the state of ghetto-Judaism. It has recorded the process of modernization which has fashioned the new Jew.

We shall attempt to survey the reactions of modern Hebrew writers to the new trends in Jewish history, the new modes of being to which the Jews have aspired during this period, bending all their energies to making a place for themselves in the world, to sharing modern civilization on terms of equality with the rest of occidental society.

with the problems involved in its own local emancipation.

German-Jewish literature produced during the period of Jewish emancipation in Germany, roughly between 1780 and 1850, was concerned almost exclusively with the implications of the process for German Jews alone. French-Jewish writings, such as one may find well represented in the *Archives Israélites* between 1840–1890, mainly seek to clarify the relationship between the French Jew and France (the first European nation to grant its Jews political and civic equality). Jewish literature in Russian, roughly from 1860 to the revolution of 1917, is predominantly concerned with the struggle of the Jewish masses in czarist Russia for the equalization of their political and civic status within the bounds of the Russian empire. In short, every linguistic unit in the polyglot Jewish literature of this modern era, except the Hebrew, tends toward a kind of Jewish territorial exclusiveness. It shows an almost complete and parochial absorption in the life of the Jew in a given country alone, with relatively little interest in Jewry as a whole. The only interest this polyglot Jewish literature seems to have in universal Jewry—in Jewry as still one people living in different lands—follows one of two rather irrelevant directions. It is either a purely philanthropic interest in the fate of the less fortunate coreligionist, such as the interest which the Western Jew often took in the unemancipated Jew of Eastern Europe; or else, it is the abstract interest in the historical Jew, the Jew of the past, which has resulted in that great body of Jewish scholarship known as *Wissenschaft des Judentums,* carried on in all fields of Jewish learning. Yet, this concentration upon the historic Jew has frequently stemmed from a conscious determination and a less conscious wish to believe that universal Jewry as an authentic entity, as one and the same people living in different lands, is actually a matter of the past.

Modern Hebrew literature alone persistently refused to become parochial, territorially exclusive in its Jewish interest. From its very beginnings in the 18th century, it retained the historical Jewish awareness that Jewry, wherever it may have its home and whatever its own local fortunes, is but part of *Keneset Yisrael,* of what the late Solomon Schechter called "catholic Israel." From its very beginnings Hebrew literature tended to evaluate the changes taking place in the emancipated Jewish life, not in terms of the Jew in one country or another, but in terms of Jewry as a whole. In 1781, Naftali Herz Wessely, writing in Hebrew in Germany, drew up a program of modernized Jewish education for Austrian Jews, a program that was ultimately adopted by Italian Jewish communities. Joseph Perl, writing in Hebrew in Galicia about 1812, urged Galician Jews toward productive labor; at the same time, however, he gloried in the first halting attempts made by Russian Jews to return to agriculture in the Ukraine. By the middle of the 19th century, Samuel David Luzzatto, an Italian Jew, was waging incessant warfare upon the earliest manifestations of the Jewish inferiority complex in all of enlightened Western Europe, rather than in his own community; and in the early sixties, the Russian Peretz Smolenskin lamented the emptiness and frigidity of Reform Jewry in Germany. Hebrew literature remained forever interested in the Jew, *qua* Jew. The universal Jew rather than the Jewish denizen of a particular state or country remained the abiding object of its study in modern times, as he had been throughout the ages. For, above all others, Hebrew writers believed and insisted that the Jew, bound as he was to seek a better and richer

life and greatly change in the pursuit of it, must still preserve his historic Jewish identity.

This is indeed the one inherent difficulty which modern
Hebrew writers have faced with increasing awareness as
the process of emancipation drew ever larger numbers of
Jews away from their rooted Jewish authenticity, assimilat-
ing them to the cultural attitudes of their non-Jewish environment. On the one hand, Hebrew writers were among
the first to call upon the Jew to enlarge his capacities for the
enjoyment of the values of modern civilization: and they
remained in the vanguard observing, recording, and stimu-
lating Jewish development in the new and generally human
direction. At the same time, however—at first less consciously, but ever more so as time went on—they were also
occupied with quite another problem: how can the Jew remain a Jew while bending so much of his energies to the
modernization of his life. How can the Jew preserve his
historical identity while all his capacities must expand in
that happy worldly existence which for centuries his predecessors had not only been denied, but had also regarded as
insignificant, as intrinsically trivial and unworthy of idealization?

This inner dilemma, inherent in modern Jewish history,
did not immediately manifest itself to the Hebrew writers
with all its implications (and, therefore, will be treated
more fully in later chapters). What is essential for the present is a clearer understanding of their attitude to the positive aspects of Jewish emancipation, as that liberating and
liberalizing process came to include ever greater numbers
of Jews. It is still a common notion that the modern period
in Jewish history may best be conceived of as a pyramid—a
pyramid whose base is Jewish political emancipation; its

center—social and economic expansion; and its apex—cultural adjustment to the non-Jewish environment with consequent deterioration of the Jewish will-to-live, or assimilationism. The popular assumption is that modern Jewry was first granted political and civic equality in country after country; that with the attainment of equal rights, Jews everywhere rose economically and socially; and that with the economic and social rise, they inevitably tended to integrate themselves into the non-Jewish cultural environment; and, therefore, also tended to lose their love for Judaism, for their own historical civilization.

It is only in very recent decades that historians have come to recognize that if the process of Jewish emancipation is at all to be represented by a pyramid, it is something of an inverted pyramid that is wanted. For actually the political emancipation of European Jewry followed upon, rather than preceded, Jewish economic expansion with its consequent cultural and—to some extent—social emancipation. Political emancipation, or the so-called equal rights granted to the Jews in any European state, generally lagged far behind their economic and cultural development in that state. It is true that Jewish emancipation coincided with the growth of the democratic state and with the spread of enlightenment in Western, Central and Eastern Europe. But Jewish emancipation also coincided with the spectacular industrialization of the Continent, with the onward march of its capitalist economic system. Historians and sociologists have fully established the contributions made by individual Jews during this period to the economic life of Europe— in finance, industry and commerce; and this economic factor proved one of the prime determinants of Jewish political emancipation in one European state after another.

When Prussian Jewry was emancipated politically in 1812, and all of German Jewry in 1869, Jews had already been playing leading roles in German commerce for many decades before. The Jews of England saw all their civic disabilities removed during the middle decades of the 19th century; but, again, for over one hundred years before their enfranchisement, they had occupied an eminent position in the economic life of the country, which was reflected both in the activities of the London stock exchange and in colonial trade. Russian-Polish Jewry achieved equal rights only with the advent of the revolution of 1917. But even in czarist Russia, Jews began as early as 1840 to play a prominent role in financial, industrial and commercial life. This ultimate political emancipation in state after state was the formal recognition of the economic expansion they had achieved much earlier.

But parallel to the economic expansion of Jewish life there was a broadening of the Jew's intellectual cravings long before Jewry anywhere was granted political equality. A strange intellectual unrest seized upon European Jewry in the first years of the 18th century—an unrest somewhat reminiscent of the spirit of the European Renaissance as it spread from Italy through France and Holland to England, in the 15th and 16th centuries. This unrest bespoke a dissatisfaction with the narrow confines of traditional Jewish intellectual endeavor, a dissatisfaction with the exclusive absorption in rabbinic lore and the intricacies of talmudic studies. A wider and more colorful intellectual life began to urge itself upon a young Jew here and there as he stooped over an old tome in the gloom of the synagogue or the talmudic academy. Such a young Jew no longer delighted in perceiving some apparent inconsistency between one early hallowed commentary on an obscure talmudic passage and another. He no longer thrilled with the awareness of having scaled dizzy intellectual heights when he had followed the subtleties of an interpretation of a rabbinic text by the dean of the academy. He began to crave secular information, and here and there he set out to find it. He dreamed of leaving "a mother and city in Israel," such as Vilna in Lithuania, in order to study medicine in Padua, Italy, as did one Judah Hurwitz, later known as "the physician." Or he left his home in Dessau, as did Moses Mendelssohn—presumably to continue his talmudic studies under the guidance of his beloved teacher who had moved to Berlin; only to find himself, some ten years later, among the leaders of non-Jewish German intellectual life in the capital of Prussia.

Indeed, the best illustration of the divergence in time between Jewish intellectual and political emancipation is to be found in the figure of this hunchbacked sage of Dessau and Berlin. When in 1744, aged fourteen or fifteen, he arrived at the gates of Berlin, he was nearly denied admission because Jews who had not been granted the necessary privilege were not permitted to live in Berlin. In fact, for almost twenty years afterward, and while already famous as a great German philosopher and master of German prose, Moses Mendelssohn was an *ausserordentlicher Schutzjude* (extra-regularly protected), that is, he was permitted to live in Berlin only because he held the position of bookkeeper with the firm of a wealthy *Schutzjude* who had that special privilege and could extend it to his employees—and that under the enlightened Frederick the Great. Even when some twenty years later Mendelssohn himself was granted this privilege in recognition of his achievements in German

philosophy and literature, he could not bequeath his right
of domicile in the Prussian capital to his wife and children,
who obtained it only after his death in 1787. And yet this
outlawed Jew was among the giants of the German intellectualism of his day. Mendelssohn was an intimate friend
of Lessing's; he was honored by Nikolai, the editor of the
famous *Bibliothek der Schönen Wissenschaften und Freien
Kuenste* and of *Briefe die neueste Litteratur betreffend*,
literary miscellanies to which he contributed his brilliant
critical and esthetic studies of European literature. The
renowned author of numerous works in metaphysics and
other branches of philosophy, he was the recipient of the
first prize awarded by the Berlin Academy for an original
philosophic treatise, in a contest in which Immanuel Kant
himself won only the second prize.

Mendelssohn was indeed the protagonist of that intellectual hunger which overtook the Jewish spiritual ghetto
in the early 18th century, greatly antedating Jewish political
enfranchisement. He was the most vivid representative of
that hunger, but far from being the only one. Actually,
upon his arrival in Berlin he found that other Jews with intellectual propensities and ambitions had preceded him,
driven by impulses similar to his own. In his first years there
he studied mathematics with one Israel of Zamostz, who
had been persecuted in his home town in Poland because of
his addiction to algebra and geometry. Mendelssohn
learned Latin from the physician Abraham Kisch of
Prague, and French and English from one of the early
Hebrew writers on science, Aaron Gomperz of Hamburg.
During the next few decades, even as early as the end of the
18th century, the number of these seekers of enlightenment
grew everywhere in the ghettos of Central and Eastern

Europe. They were to multiply beyond counting during the next hundred years. Everywhere the urge for intellectual emancipation preceded political emancipation by many weary decades.

In the beginning Hebrew writers not only preached the urgency of intellectual expansion but made strenuous efforts to supply the necessary literature. They produced popular works in the natural sciences, mathematics, history and geography, philosophy, in ethics and esthetics—all to fill the crying need for popular education at first in Central and later in Eastern Europe. From the middle of the 18th century in Germany and Holland to the last quarter of the 19th in Poland and Russia, Hebrew writers were primarily engaged in preaching what is known as Haskalah, Enlightenment, to ever widening sections of Jewry. Among the most permanent features of Hebrew Haskalah was culture, *hokhmah,* which was to be attained through secular education. This was a term frequently encountered in the first one hundred years of modern Hebrew letters, although the faith displayed in its implications now seems pathetic and naive. For *hokhmah,* as used by Haskalah writers, meant no more than the acquisition by Jews of an amount of knowledge of science, history, languages and literature that is today approximately covered by a college education. Yet so completely excluded from secular education had the Jewish ghetto been for centuries, that even this pathetic ideal of popular education for the Jewish masses pointed to a stirring yearning for a revitalized Jewish existence. The self-contained complacency of ghetto civilization had come face to face with a crisis. Jewry in ever increasing numbers craved what Haskalah literature called the "expansion of the intellect"; and one of the earliest injunctions of modern

Hebrew literature is "not to drive the Jew away from the urgently needed sciences." Hebrew writers, therefore, even in one of the earliest stages of Haskalah—in Germany, 1781–1820—produced not only poetry, literary criticism, fiction, drama, travelogues: works, in short, aiming to satisfy the esthetic needs of the Hebrew reader; they produced also numerous works of a more utilitarian character which sought to cultivate a rational understanding of the universe, of society, and of the Jew's own place in the world. Popular indeed were those numerous works of science and philosophy, history and geography, education and pedagogy, social studies and journalism. The fact is that from the very beginning Hebrew writers branched out into almost every field of rational inquiry as well as of imaginative writing; and most of their more significant works went through many editions. These two facts speak for the upsurge of the new intellectual curiosity which characterized the age and was destined to characterize it for more than a hundred years.

Yet, it would be an error to overemphasize secular education as the be-all and end-all of the Haskalah period, and as the chief preoccupation of its writers. They had a far greater purpose in view—none other than the emergence of the "modern Jew," a purpose to which secular education was simply the basic prerequisite. The modern Jew was not only to encompass in himself the best qualities, skills and insights of the Western world and be capable of living a well-balanced life on earth, he was also to retain with the deepest sense of integration the distinctive qualities of the historically fashioned Jew. The modern Jew is the descendant of forefathers who some two hundred years ago began to act upon their impulsions toward that worldly self-fulfillment so long denied them by the ghetto: impulsions which were to result in immense expansions of Jewish life along lines biological, geographic, social and economic, as well as cultural. It is a fact that during this period the Jews increased about three times as rapidly as European society as a whole; so that from a people numbering no more than about one and one-half millions at the end of the 17th century, Jewry grew to about sixteen and one-half millions in the years immediately preceding the advent of Hitlerism. It was during this period, in the 19th and 20th centuries, that Jewry, which in the 18th century was largely concentrated in Central and Eastern Europe, saw four to five millions of its numbers migrate to all parts of the world overseas in answer to the call of a better and happier life on earth. In response to this call the Jews became in a relatively short time one of the most urbanized peoples in the world, with a correspondingly expanded economic life. It was the lure of worldly happiness that had wrenched them out of their set, time-honored, rabbinical ghetto civilization and opened up to them the vast vistas of the cultural world.

It is of course true that Hebrew literature has chiefly tended to further Jewish cultural expansion, although an attempt will be made in the following chapters to discuss the vital interest Hebrew literature has constantly maintained in the more material expansions of Jewish life. What should be stressed here, however, is that modern Hebrew literature from its earliest period on has been in the vanguard of the Jewish quest for a more widely expanded Jewish civilization. Both aspects of the ideal, the universally humanistic as well as the Jewish, were always equally close to its heart. "In its earliest period"—1781–1820—Joseph Klausner writes of modern Hebrew literature, "it filled a

vital need in the life of our people at the decisive hour of
its transformation, beginning with the emergence from the
ghetto. . . . It is not true that modern Hebrew literature
trampled underfoot all the sanctities of Israel, as Hebrew
and non-Hebrew writing Jewish authors have charged for
the past sixty-seventy years, from the days of the Love of
Zion movement to our day. The Hebrew writers of the
Haskalah period were not extreme in their views: the historical tradition of their medium, of Hebrew, the religio-
national language, did not let them assume an utterly negative attitude toward the religio-national tradition. In
general, almost no Hebrew author dared to ridicule the
doctrines of the Jewish religion; it was only superstitions
and trivial folkways that were frequently the targets of
attack. Hebrew authors, even those of the Haskalah period,
had come to build rather than to destroy. The destroyers
were Jewish authors who wrote in European languages. On
the other hand, those who wrote Hebrew, with all their
aspiration for light and enlightenment, sought ways to
bring into accord intellectual enlightenment and religion,
the present and past. The sacred language and Jewish history itself, however secularized and reinterpreted by these
Hebrew writers, compelled them to treat tradition more
reverently, whether consciously or instinctively. For they
ever remained with their people, with the folk. The assimilationist Jews always were the wealthy and the holders
of university diplomas, those who adopted the language and
culture of the state which afforded them greater wealth
and honor. With the Hebrew authors remained the middle
and the poorer classes in Jewry . . . so that modern Hebrew literature has, to a great extent, been a folk-litera-
ture."

We shall take up in a later chapter the tragic situation

which Hebrew writers had to deal with repeatedly in one country after another; namely, that as the Jewish masses, the middle and poorer classes, rose economically and socially, they tended to join the ranks of "the wealthy and the holders of university diplomas"; so that Jewish folk life was everywhere urged toward secular expansion as its main goal, with little or no surviving interest in the preservation of the historic Jewish identity. One fact is important for the moment. The ideals preached by modern Hebrew literature in its very first stages voiced the hunger for a fuller human life in the heart of the simple Jewish folk. It spoke for all Jewry and especially for that East European Jewry which in the 18th century was one mass of semistarved, bleeding and humiliated humanity. The Hebrew authors of the early Haskalah period were a relatively small group of men in Holland, Germany, Austria, and here and there in Southwestern Russia. But this handful of poets, essayists and popularizers of Western science, art and philosophy did not speak for themselves, or for scattered individual Jews like themselves, when they stressed the desperate necessity of enriching the life of the Jew with new content. They were doing something far more profound than this; they also gave rational expression and form to strongly felt needs which were already expressing themselves in more emotional, non-literary, and even anti-intellectualist ways. The pietistic movement of Hasidism, the sensualist nihilistic tenets of the Frankists—these were strikingly opposed to each other in immediate purpose and means; yet both represented the ferment which was everywhere bursting the constricting bands of outworn formalism and reaching out for a freer life to which the new literature was giving a rational formulation.

Jewish historians of the 19th century, including the

great Heinrich Graetz himself, not only condemned the movement started by Jacob Frank as a crude mixture of charlatanism, superstition and licentiousness; they were also mildly disdainful of Hasidism, utterly failing to see even in this superb religious and social movement the stirring awakening of the Jewish masses to a new realization of the glories of man's life on earth. It may still be difficult to regard the Frankist philosophy as symptomatic of that awakening, to connect the positive elements in the Jewish renascence with the anarchical Frankist revolt against ritualism and legalism, as it found expression in the sermons addressed by Jacob Frank to his thousands of followers. Yet in the light of what has been said concerning the longings for the new which agitated Jewry in the 18th century, who can fail to hear them resoundingly echoed even in the iconoclastic maxims of a Jacob Frank? A graphic illustration of this point is provided by some of Frank's preachments to his followers: (1) "Man is born for happiness"; (2) "What has been has been: now a new time has come. We shall no longer busy ourselves with that which has so long engaged us. Henceforth we shall study military tactics only"; (3) "We must trample down all the laws that have existed heretofore"; (4) "Heed what I say unto you. If there is one among you who keeps in his heart the least memory of the old studies—he surely shall perish, he and all about him. For our destination is a place which will not suffer law and ritual; for these carry with them only death, while we are marching toward life"; (5) "I have therefore come unto you in Poland to do away with all beliefs and [religious] customs, for I wish to bring life to the world."

But the Jewish mentality is even today reluctant to read

the signs of the time in these semi-Nietzschean pronounce-
ments. Yet such scholars as S. I. Hurwitz, Meir Balaban,
Zalman Rubashov, and, particularly Gershom Scholem,
have in recent years delved into the heart of the Frankist
movement to illumine it also as one of the precursors of
the Jewish renascence. It is at least vital to remember what
Gershom Scholem has observed concerning the underlying
principles of the "spiritual world" of all the post-Sab-
batean* trends and sects in the course of about one hundred
and fifty years, beginning roughly with the last quarter of
the 17th century and on to the end of the 18th. To quote
Scholem: "The crisis that took place in modern Judaism in
the decades following the opening up of the ghetto had
already been prepared from within in the obscure recesses
of the Jewish mind and in the sanctum sanctorum of mystic
doctrine and of the Kabbalah itself. Within the ghetto
walls there had already emerged individuals and groups
whose real life and conceptions were completely transformed, for all their external preservation of the [tradi-
tional] Jewish forms of life. In the period preceding the
French Revolution the necessary historic conditions were
still lacking for the transformation of this invisible force
into a manifestly revolutionary drive. This force, therefore,
remained a cause of inward revolt in the hidden areas of
Jewish consciousness and Jewish life. But we shall greatly
err, if we assume that there is no connection between the
former and the latter. The yearnings for self-liberation
which found such tragic expression in the nihilistic doctrine
of the Sabbateans do not point to destructive forces only
operating within it. On the contrary, the historian is obliged

---

* The Sabbatean movement was initiated by the pseudo-Messiah Sab-
batai Zevi.

to see the positive element in this negativism, the construc-
tive aspirations inherent in the very destructiveness [of
post-Sabbateanism]—to discern those aspirations behind
all the veils, behind all the abominable and licentious acts
of the movement."

Surely, Hasidism, at least, has vindicated itself in recent
decades as that stirring to a new life in Jewry which literally
swept the Jewish masses off their feet long before they came
to register the impact of the Haskalah, or of modern Hebrew literature, for that matter. Who today at all acquainted
with the teachings of its founder, the Baal Shem Tov, and
his disciples, fails to realize that Hasidism was the great call
to life sounded in Jewry, in East European Jewry, before
that call assumed rational meaning for it in Hebrew literature? To stress this point is but to emphasize a truism. And
yet Hasidism was not merely a religious and mystical movement which attracted only the élite. It was also—and above
all—a social movement. Within a few decades of its annunciation, in mid-18th century, Hasidism had intoxicated
hundreds of thousands of Jews because its great message to
them was that of joy and inner freedom. And it continued
to affect millions in successive generations because its fundamental insistence was on the dignity of the human personality and the privilege of being alive, of thrilling to the
glories of the God-given world. True enough, it was a religious doctrine. But it not only revealed the immanence of
God in trees and water, in color and sound, in thought and
feeling; it lighted up the worlds of nature and of the soul
with a sense of the divine which made physical nature and
the human personality sources of endless ecstasy. It not
only stressed worship; it also stressed the song and the
dance. It venerated the unfolding of personality in action,

speech, thought and feeling. Of course it remained as rigorously orthodox in its sanctification of all the minutiae of the Shulhan Arukh as was the traditional Judaism against which it unconsciously rebelled. But its main emphasis was upon the sacredness of life.

That emphasis was the cry of the age, and it remained for modern Hebrew literature to state it rationally: to give it clearer utterance, and to direct it toward goals and objectives which Hasidism, naturally enough, little envisaged. Moses Hayyim Luzzatto, Moses Mendelssohn, Naftali Herz Wessely, the fathers of modern Hebrew literature, and the scores of their followers who shaped this literature, were the men who in more conscious terms sought to interpret to the Jew the meaning of his need for a new life as Jew and as human being. As the implications of the struggle emerged in ever greater complexity, the purely religious tones of the call became ever more muffled; its overtones frequently appeared strident, ill-harmonized with traditional Judaism. But no attempt to understand even these disharmonies in modern Hebrew literature is possible without a realization of the relationship between this new body of Hebrew letters, mainly secular in character, and the religious Jewish folk life from which it sprang. The complications in which modern Hebrew literature found itself involved in consequence of this situation created a dilemma which will be considered in succeeding chapters.

CHAPTER II

The Dilemma of
Haskalah Literature

HASKALAH literature is generally thought of as covering one hundred years in the history of modern Hebrew letters, from 1781 to 1881. And this century of Hebraic creative activity is further subdivided into three periods. The first, 1781–1830, is called the period of rationalism. It is supposedly in that age that Hebrew writers championed the cause of enlightenment, of the secularization of Jewish life; supposedly at the same time, these writers also sought to defend the new secular ideals against the opposition they were bound to provoke in orthodox Jewry. The second period, 1830–1850, is called the period of romanticism. This is commonly held to describe those years in Haskalah literature when Hebrew authors, influenced by a revived consciousness of the true worth of the Jewish past, nostalgically bent their efforts to harmonize the new secular ideology with the spirit of traditional Judaism. Finally, the third period, 1850–1880, is known as the period of realism: in this time Hebrew authors are thought to have developed a ruthlessly sober sense of the anomalies of Jewish life in the ghetto, and to have begun to wage offensive warfare upon Jewish traditionalism. The assumption is that in these last thirty years of the Haskalah, Hebrew writers regarded Jewish traditionalism as the main cause of all that was unwholesome in Jewish ghetto existence; their onslaughts upon Jewish traditionalism, therefore, became rabid.

Whether or not such a neat division of Haskalah letters into clearly marked-off periods is defensible from a literary point of view is a question which is beyond the scope of this book. From a purely social point of view, however, there can be no doubt that Haskalah literature—perhaps all of modern Hebrew literature, for that matter—was at all times a peculiar blending of rationalism, romanticism, and realism. The rationalistic element was dominant insofar as the Jew was incessantly urged to apply reason in appraising his life: in diagnosing the ills from which he suffered, as well as in devising ways and means to correct them. Such a diagnosis of necessity meant a courageous and frequently an unflinching examination of the realities of Jewish life; so that the writers who urged honest self-examination inevitably tended toward realism throughout the period. Yet, strangely enough, Haskalah literature never quite ceased to be romantic. For all its rationalism and realism, it remained incurably romantic because it was always inspired by a naive faith, faith in the essential nobility of human life, faith in man, and faith in the Jew's own power to survive as a Jew, as a distinct ethnic being even when he had lost much of his ghetto otherworldliness.

Rationalism, realism, and romanticism, as different trends in style and manner, might each from time to time predominate in the different literary periods of the age of the Enlightenment. Yet from a social point of view these three were never at any time mutually exclusive. In this respect Haskalah letters always remained eclectic. They were forever intoxicated with a thirst for life and with an optimistic faith in the capacities of the Jew to shape his life into something ideally worthwhile, if only the Jew ministered to his needs rationally, realistically. Indeed, the character of modern Hebrew literature, the Haskalah period included, can best be understood in terms of the humanism to which European civilization began to waken five or six hundred years ago in the age of the Renaissance. Jewish life was overtaken by the ideals of humanism some three hundred years later than non-Jewish Europe. But the reflection of these yearnings and ideals in Hebrew letters cannot be evaluated unless viewed in the light of the earlier occidental awakening from scholasticism, from medievalism.

In the history of the European Renaissance, the term humanism is generally related to the Latin *humanitas,* the Greco-Roman culture to the study of which the humanists dedicated themselves. In its wider implications, the term humanism should be related to *humanus,* man, for it was man who became the all-absorbing object of interest to the protagonists of the European Renaissance. They spoke of and for man, man on earth. As against the ideals of medieval otherworldliness and asceticism, humanism insisted on man's right, more, man's duty to live a full life. Neither the physical lusts of the Renaissance society nor the sensuous wealth of its art and poetry can be understood unless we bear in mind this new emphasis on the importance of life as an end in itself. Intellectually, too, man became the measure of all things. Humanism stressed man's right to inquire into his own nature as well as into the nature of the world he lived in, rather than fall back upon the traditional creed and dogma which for over a thousand years provided all the answers to all possible questions concerning these matters. It was as a result of this emphasis upon the right and duty of reasonable man to seek and investigate the truth that modern science and philosophy developed. And reason was extolled to even greater heights. For it was man rather than theology or ecclesiastic ethics that was henceforth to help man shape his moral destiny. The struggle against the divine rights of kings, the growth of democracy, the ever wider understanding of social betterment—all ultimately sprang from "humanism," from the new self-confidence which man had come to have in himself as man, as the rational being normally compelled to use reason, the noblest faculty in his possession.

It is therefore striking enough to find Haskalah literature also preaching the supremacy of reason, of man's power to think for himself, as the most efficacious means at the disposal of the Jew to shape for himself a better life in the world. True enough, in common usage the term Haskalah meant something more limited and practical than the abstract adulation of reason. From its earliest inception in the second half of the 18th century to the frustration of the movement about 1880, Haskalah did not always readily suggest the wider intellectual concept inherent in such equivalents of the term as the English "enlightenment," or even the German *Aufklärung*. In fact, throughout the century of its widest prevalence Haskalah meant mainly education: instruction in the European languages, especially the official language of the country in which the Jewish community in question lived, and in the natural sciences; vocational training with a view to the improvement of the occupational distribution of the poverty-stricken masses in Eastern Europe; and last but not least the westernization of

folkways and manners. It was in this sense of applied Jewish mass education, or re-education, that the concept was
used by Hebrew writers.

In fact, one has only to read Isaac Satanov's panegyrics
to the intellect, to appreciate the perennial religious adoration accorded to it by Haskalah. In cadences strongly reminiscent of the praise of wisdom found in such passages of
the Bible as Proverbs, chapter 8, or Job, chapter 28, and in
any number of verses in the apocryphal "Wisdom of Solomon," Satanov frequently rhapsodizes on this theme, as in
the following quotation: "Because God loved Wisdom, he
adopted her as his daughter. He himself lovingly brought
her up. Before he made heaven and earth, she was his de-
light; before the mountains were born, ere the hills were
formed. Because he willed to span heaven and earth, to do
good to his creatures, to whom he would thus reveal the
beatific splendor of his kingdom, he called upon Wisdom
to present herself before him, and to her he said, 'My
daughter, it is my intent to rear a dwelling place that will be
inhabited by a multitude of beings. It is my will to establish
my throne, and have my footstool upon the earth—therefore, be thou with me to give me sweet counsel. For I shall
do nothing without thee . . .' And she was henceforth
with the King at his work. He took counsel with her; how
to spread the sky with skill, and give the stars their measure-
ments and rhythms . . . then, because God loved man, he
sent Wisdom to walk upon the earth, that her delightful
employ be with man, who would choose her in order to survive unto great salvation. . . ."

Students of 18th century European literature will recognize in this passage familiar echoes of the anthropocentric
deism of the period with its inveterate faith in the God-

given human intellect, which, if wisely used, would eventually establish paradise on earth. Undoubtedly, the optimism of early Haskalah literature was greatly influenced by the progressivism of the period, especially as it was reflected in English and French literature. No doubt, the cosmopolitanism of the age, which drew its inspiration from the American and French Revolutions with their stirring annunciation of man's coming into his own at last, also helped to nurture in Haskalah literature its faith in man. Emulating this forward-looking *homo sapiens,* the Jew, too, would prove worthy of sharing the blessings of the earthly paradise cultivated at will by the intellect. The 19th century with its continued "march of progress" only strengthened this optimism in Haskalah letters. Yet the emotional optimism in which Haskalah literature was steeped bespoke a hunger for a life which was much more characteristic of the European Renaissance. It was this enriched happy life that Haskalah literature set up as the ideal for the Jew, too. The Jew also could attain it, if once he determined to become the clear-sighted master of his destiny rather than continue as the slave of hidebound tradition.

Few spokesmen of the Haskalah, writing in Hebrew, dared to assert as bluntly as Solomon Maimon did in his autobiography that Jews had suffered unspeakably in the past only because of their reluctance to change. For, he wrote, "only their obscurantism, their antagonism to implications of sound character and wholesome reform, has been the cause of all the ills that befell them." That the Jew must rid himself of this traditional attitude became the explicit credo of all Haskalah literature. The Jew could and must begin to share in the fruits of human progress with the rest of civilized humanity. It all depended upon him, upon his readiness to use his intelligence. The Jew by his own will could reshape his world, could channel life in a new direction. Indeed, the social optimism of Haskalah literature in the course of its hundred years is best summed up by Judah Leib Gordon in the famous stanza of his exhortation to Russian Jewry (written in 1863 and published in 1866):

> "Awake, my people! How long will you sleep?
> Night has taken flight, the sun shines bright.
> Awake, lift up your eyes and look about—
> Become aware of time and place."

The idealization of the intellect as the most trustworthy assurance of bliss, accessible not only to the individual Jew but to Jewry as a whole, imparted to Haskalah literature a quality of naive, simple faith which seems cloying to the modern reader. Yet that naive, simple faith contrasted sharply with the uncompromising realism with which this same literature, for over a hundred years, analyzed its Jewish environment—in Eastern Europe above all. There is an inner cleavage between the vision of the good life that inspired most of these writings and the awareness of the realities of that Jewish environment. This divergence between the ideal and the real can be traced as an almost straight line of demarcation between the poetry of the Haskalah period and its prose.

Let us look briefly at Haskalah poetry, first, in its social aspects. Its ideal is the well-rounded intellectual and emotional personality which the Jew must develop in contradistinction to that anemic otherworldly being, the ghetto-Jew. This ideal Jew is a being whose physical desires are as refined as his spiritual aspirations. He lives a noble emotional life, loves nature, is sensitively attuned to the beauty of woman, to her spiritual attractiveness, of course, above all; he thrills to the joys of perfect friendship, forever emulating the David-and-Jonathan relationship; he ever savors anew the love of his fellow man; he instinctively responds to poetry and music. And, intellectually, this ideal Jew is just as wideawake and well balanced. His sensibility vibrates to the glories of the universe and his mind organizes his impressions into a harmonious philosophic system. Science, which he ardently studies, only helps him soar into the higher regions of pleasurable metaphysics. First: multifarious nature; next: God, who is ever well intentioned; last, and not least: man, endowed with an imperishable moral soul; these are the permanent objects of his wonder-stricken inquiry. What this perfectly felicitous Jew does for a living hardly ever seems worth considering. Indeed, insofar as this question existed at all in the subconscious of Haskalah poets, they seem to suggest that this protagonist of the ideal life should lead a bucolic existence, tending flocks or walking behind the plough. This idyllic solution of the submerged question which the poetry of the period may have asked concerning the economic status of the emergent new Jew is not necessarily facetious in its implications. It undoubtedly expressed the budding love of nature which was quite a novelty to the ghetto-Jew; and the equally new urge toward agriculture, which was preached by Haskalah prose writers also, but in more concrete terms in answer to economic needs of the Jews. Nevertheless, this poetry, in its pursuit of the ideal life, is little concerned with the crass realities of Jewish subsistence in the abysmal poverty of the ghetto. The life that the poets of Haskalah visualize for the Jew is indeed a kind of Arcadia. Leading his flocks in ever green pastures, by ever limpid brooks, the dreamed-of Jew

How characteristic of all Haskalah poetry is the following paraphrase of a passage from this play: Honesty, berated by Populace and hopelessly lovelorn, pours out his heart: "The shepherd lad, no happier lot than his may be found on earth; lowly are his ambitions, no grandeur does he seek; tending the flock by the spring is his only concern, and then some tasting of its milk. He sees the sun rising red in the east—itself an undying well of joy. Blithely he keeps in step with the sheep as they graze; he plays the reed while his eyes discern each blade of grass on his mountains, and his lips utter praise to their creator. How blissful he is! How good and sweet all his days!—For changeable as the world's fortunes may be, he unwittingly scorns fickle luck; —and he is happy in his poverty, for he never covets wealth; envy and glory do not oppress his heart. His little watch-house is better than a royal palace; his staff and bag more precious than elegant raiment. The young girl Fate will bring him will surely afford him joy. . . . For their lot in life they (and their offspring) will render each moment a thousand thanks to their Benefactor."

Add to such pastoral effusiveness some of the grandiloquence of discourse on the virtues of the soul, in its never ending aspirations toward the sublime, the good and the true, and you have all the weary cantos of an epic by Wessely, "all of which," to quote the author's introduction, "recites the praise of the Lord and his might and his wonders wrought on behalf of our fathers when he led them forth from the land of Egypt and brought them to Mount Sinai." Set these pathetically pure yearnings for the life of the spirit in the framework of the more readable verse of the period, and you have a fair notion of Haskalah poetry at its best.

What a gulf separates the mood of Haskalah poetry from that of its prose! Reason, indeed, is what Haskalah prose also holds up as the key to happiness which the ghetto-Jew must forge himself, if he is to achieve that happiness. But, unlike the poets who sing ecstatically of the ideal Jew to come, the prose writers are almost exclusively aware of the real Jew whom they seek to help in the ghetto. As early as 1781 Haskalah prose reflects the shabby realities of Jewish economic and cultural life, mainly in Galicia and Poland; and those realities, affecting ever greater numbers of Jews of Eastern Europe, continue to be the aching preoccupation of Hebrew writers all through the 19th century. Except for a relatively small group, the upper bourgeoisie, Eastern European Jewry throughout the period of its struggle for emancipation remains a mass of impoverished millions who eke out their semistarved lives without any sense of economic security from day to day, from decade to decade. All through this period the great majority of East European Jews are miserably poor shopkeepers, peddlers, agents, and porters; plus, of course, the similarly ragged hierarchy of "professional Jews," the celebrated "holy vessels" of the period: the Rabbi and the Shohet, the Shammash and the Hazzan, the Melammed and the Shadhan. Culturally, also, Jewish backwardness, Jewish obscurantism, as the Haskalah writers were wont to call it, is appalling. All through the Haskalah period, as for centuries before it, the school continues to regard as heretical the most elementary instruction in secular subjects. Jewish children, for reasons presumably religious, are forbidden to study the language of the country or the rudiments of history and geography. The slightest deviation from ritual is considered apostasy. Superstition reigns supreme. When capitalist industrialization begins to expand in the Russian empire by the middle of the 19th century, individual Jews in Russia and in Poland rise from the desperate poverty of the ghetto to a position of greater wealth and wider cultural opportunities. In the latter decades a developing class-conscious Jewish proletariat also begins to grope for a freer economic and cultural life. Nevertheless, millions of Jews throughout the 19th century are still subjected to those socio-economic and cultural conditions which Haskalah literature inevitably condemns as subhuman, and to change which it seeks to rouse the Jew out of his lethargic sense of helplessness.

There is hardly a prose writer to be found in this period who is not concerned with this tragic state of the Jewish masses. But the most vivid illustration of the exclusively social character of Haskalah prose is provided by Mendele Mocher Seforim, who only in the last decades of the 19th century described the subhuman aspects of Jewish ghetto realities in his truly monumental works. Hard-bitten and excessively satirical as Mendele's penetrating studies of the Jewish ghetto may seem to us today, they virtually are the museum of ghetto misery, of Jewish realia in Eastern Europe, much as Cervantes' *Don Quixote* is the epitomization of a degenerate Spanish chivalry, or Gogol's *Dead Souls* the immortal representation of decadent Russian feudalism. Mendele gave allegorical names to the three Jewish towns in the Pale of Settlement which constituted the scenes of his novels. But these names forcibly suggest the realities of the ghetto during the Haskalah period. "Beggars' Town," "Idlers' Town," and "Dunce Town" are place-names which should readily evoke a vivid impression of the true conditions of the Jewish ghetto even in the mind of one who has not read Mendele's work. The prethe presses. The Heder and the Yeshivah are variously appraised, more tolerantly in the early decades of Haskalah, but more scornfully later on. Of course the Jewish child must continue to receive a traditionally Jewish education, but the explicit emphasis is placed upon making education both secular and vocational. The full development of the Jewish personality is finally urged along lines which today may even strike the reader as both ludicrous and pathetic. Haskalah prose is very explicit, for instance, in its clamor for the improvement of Jewish manners, Jewish garb and Jewish peculiarities of speech and deportment. In short, Haskalah prose is pedagogic, socially educational. Not only in pseudophilosophic or publicistic treatises, but also in fiction, in the fable, the story and the novel, these authors seldom if ever lost sight of the purely tutorial function of their social mission.

Naturally enough, therefore, Haskalah prose writers displayed an implicit faith in reason, in the supremacy of reason in the new European world as well as in the Jew's own intellectual capacities to cure the ills from which he suffers. The pathetic assumption of the whole period was that if only the Jews in Eastern Europe consented to change their ghetto ways, they would automatically come to share in the blessings of progress with their non-Jewish neighbors. There was a general conviction that non-Jewish society had definitely changed its attitude toward the Jew; that medieval bigotry and prejudice had completely vanished, and that the Jew was being sincerely welcomed by enlightened society. Enlightened society, therefore, must be quite ready also to grant full equality to the Jew in Eastern Europe, if only he ceased to be his frightfully outlandish medieval self. The blind faith of Haskalah spokesmen in the liberalism, the humaneness of the new progressive Europe pathetically colors the literature of the period. According to their interpretation of the new European mood, it was Jewish backwardness alone that barred the Jew from joining the brotherhood of man. He must, therefore, first of all be persuaded to open his eyes to the perverseness of his own ways. Once his eyes had been opened he would naturally tend to Europeanize himself from within and come into his rightful inheritance with the rest of European society from without. Jewish cultural segregation was the cause of Jewish misery. That segregation must therefore first be broken down by persuading the Jew to see the tragic results of his adamantine clinging to the past, to a tradition as much encrusted in superstition as it was steeped in pure religion, which was as much ossified ritualism as it was exalted spirituality.

In 1863, Moshe Leib Lilienblum could still write as follows: "We are in great distress. A rank, poisonous air chokes us. Erroneous systems of thought and nonsensical patterns of behavior have so woven themselves into our life that they have been absorbed into our bodies and minds, our veins and blood. Yet all these are insignificant in comparison with the idleness and helplessness that encompass us. Idleness and helplessness have lowered our sense of dignity, and with cruel, terrible suffering have crushed millions of Jews—each one individually in terms of his capacities, worth and station in life. If there were not among us myriads of idlers, ne'er-do-wells, *batlanim,* that is, people who are incapable of earning a livelihood for themselves and for their families by decent craftsmanship or expert knowledge, our spiritual state, too, would not be corrupt. A man who necessarily lives in the world of reality and action cannot afford to prefer fantasy and nonsensical behavior to the practical demands of life. If, therefore, we were not so steeped in idleness, we should find ourselves compelled from time to time to set aside our fallacious systems of thought and all our intellectual aberrations, because of the exigencies of living and acting."

Haskalah writers are not always so explicit in attributing what Lilienblum calls "Jewish indulgence of the fantastic," in the cultural and even the religious sense, to Jewish poverty and enforced idleness. But all of them seek to cure these two ills by waking the Jew to what Lilienblum calls "a life of action." For they all ultimately represent the point of view which he states more succinctly in another essay, characteristically entitled "The World of Chaos": "Although Jews are given to complicated calculations in the world of commerce, they are fantastic in their contemplation of any world other than commerce. They disregard life in their preference for the imaginary. Because of fantasy, life in this world seems of no importance to them." It is here, in this ceaseless call "to life in this world," that Haskalah prose meets Haskalah poetry. It is at one with it in its attempt to identify "life in this world" with "the life of reason."

In the name of reason Haskalah prose writers first use suasion in their appeal to the Jew to broaden his life culturally. They never tire of reminding him that the best authorities of Jewish religious civilization—the talmudic sages above all—never regarded secular education as inconsistent with the study of the Torah. The absolute legitimacy of the study of science, mathematics, astronomy, and even of foreign languages, is repeatedly proved by pointing out talmudic allusions to the real or assumed proficiency in

these fields of the greatest Tannaim and Amoraim. In fact,
rabbinical authority is frequently cited to prove that a
thorough knowledge of the law even requires a well-
rounded scientific education. For how can one understand
the minutiae of the laws governing Kashrut without a
thorough knowledge of zoology and anatomy? or the laws
governing agricultural ritual without botany and agron-
omy? or the rules for fixing the new moon and all the dates
of all the festivals without astronomy? Much of the zeal of
these Hebrew writers for Jewish history and biography and
for extensive research in Bible, Talmud, and medieval
Jewish poetry and philosophy, stems from the need to prove
that the greatest protagonists of Judaism were intellectual
giants who never feared secular information and who therefore enriched themselves and Judaism by the ardent pursuit of the sciences, of linguistics, and metaphysical speculation. The same appeal to Jewish history is made, in the
name of reason, whenever Haskalah prose writers seek to
drive home the urgency of training young Jews in the arts
and crafts, or of restoring Jews to agriculture. Countless
talmudic passages are exploited to prove the high regard in
which manual labor was held by the rabbis. Names of Tannaim and Amoraim who were shoemakers, blacksmiths,
weavers and what not are constantly cited for the emula-
tion of the modern Jew. Surely, the essential nobility of
the agricultural life is fully borne out by the intimate connection with the law of Moses as well as with much of talmudic literature.

Even the insistence upon the building up of a wholesome
physical and spiritual personality is backed up by traditional texts. It is not commonly known that the first literary
attempts of Moses Mendelssohn were made, albeit for a

brief while, in Hebrew. In 1750, he began publishing his *Kohelet Musar,* of which only four issues appeared, all of them containing exclusively his own essays in poetic prose, and all of them arguing the ideals of the humanized Jew. The first issue, dedicated to a study of the ennobling effect of the beauties of nature upon man, was introduced with a well-known talmudic quotation as its motto: "He who walks out in the days of Nisan [early spring] and sees trees in blossom, must pronounce a benediction: 'Blessed is He who has not omitted a thing in the world!' "

Yet even a summary description of Haskalah prose would be incomplete if it conveyed the impression that its contents were only mildly didactic and benevolently based upon traditional Jewish conceptions. A far more significant aspect was its biting satire—a mode which was much cultivated and which provided some of the most vigorous writing of the period. It was dictated as much by an artistic sense as by purely didactic aims. Its vehicle was usually fiction, the short story or the novel, whose appeal was less to the intellect than to the emotions and the imagination. Some remarkable satirical poetry also was published, especially in the last two decades of the period. Most notable in this genre is Judah Leib Gordon, who in the last twenty years of his creative life dedicated himself almost exclusively to the realistic presentation of ghetto life. Yet the imaginative writers, too, proved themselves vehement preachers of rational social thinking. It was not Joseph Perl alone that castigated the crude superstitions and vulgarities of Galician folk-Hasidism in his parodies of the hasidic tales of wonder and miracle. Isaac Erter, a consummate artist, in his finely executed sketches of the same Galician milieu, also brought to the surface every moral

defection which lurked under the guise of extreme ghetto
religiosity. Peretz Smolenskin, a prolific and stirring novelist, succeeded in painting a veritable panorama of Jewish
life in 19th century White Russia and the Ukraine. Yet his
strong social feeling turns all his pathos into a violent ar-
raignment of Jewish poverty and orthodox bigotry. Abraham Mapu is best known for his novels of biblical history
around the time of the fall of the Northern Kingdom; but
he also becomes the satirical analyst of Jewish obscurantism in his longest novel, "The Painted Vulture," another
wide canvas on which is portrayed the life of Lithuanian
Jewry of his day. As we have seen, the satirization of all
that is shabby, supine and sterile in Jewish ghettoism is one
of the main inspirations of Mendele Mocher Seforim himself, the first truly gigantic figure in modern Jewish letters,
even when measured by the best standards of continental
literature. Satire, indeed, is the mark of Haskalah fiction,
even as romantic rationalism characterizes its poetry.

To sum up, Haskalah prose aspires to the same ideal
Jew as does the poetry. But Haskalah poetry celebrates this
ideal character as if he already existed. The prose treatment
of the theme, by contrast, is sadly sober, even embittered by
the realization of the great distance between the Jew as he
is and the Jew as he should be. Thus, Haskalah poetry can
afford to remain exaltedly cloistered in its visions of individualistic aggrandizement, while Haskalah prose is not
only manifestly social, but also violently realistic. While
the poet blissfully indulges his dreams of the ultimate goal,
the fiction writer is conscious of its remoteness. Insofar as
the unemancipated Jew retains his distinct Jewish identity,
he is not yet the ideal human being envisioned by Haskalah
writers. Haskalah poets, for the most part, forget this fact,

while Haskalah prose writers forever and painfully remember it.

This, indeed, is the contradiction of the literature of the period—the dilemma of the Haskalah. Insofar as its humanistic ideals are realized, the emergent individual Jew tends to find his fulfillment in the non-Jewish civilization to which he comes to belong either through external political, or through internal social and cultural, emancipation. On the other hand, the large masses of unemancipated Jews respond but slowly to the aspirations urged upon them by Haskalah writers.

Haskalah literature begins everywhere by propagating a philosophy of humanistic expansion among a Jewry confined to the ghetto. Its message is welcomed by some; but it is spurned by most, who regard it as sheer heresy, an onslaught upon the traditional sanctities of Judaism. But what is equally tragic is that those Jews who are emancipated, who do become enlightened and embrace the brave new world, very soon are absorbed by that larger world and tend to disappear as Jews.

The contradiction between the ideal Jew of Haskalah poetry and the real Jew of Haskalah prose fundamentally meant that the literature of the period never asked itself seriously enough the one question which Hebrew letters have been asking for the last seventy years: "How can the Jew survive as a Jew, distinct and distinctive, once he comes to share fully the cultural non-Jewish environment of the country in which he lives?" This question which has haunted Hebrew literature since 1880 was sensed but vaguely by Haskalah letters.

CHAPTER III

The Transvaluation of Values

HASKALAH writers were conscious of the gulf that separated the real Jew depicted by the prose from the ideal Jew envisioned in the poetry; yet they never quite understood that the fateful gulf was unbridgeable under the circumstances. We must, therefore, try to understand why Hebrew literature for so long a time failed to appreciate more concretely the elusive nature of the ideal Jew it sought. Its goal was the realization of the new Jew who would be humanistically expanded yet would retain his own colorful historical identity. Why, then, did this goal remain unattainable?

Much of the literature produced in Hebrew before 1880 is often thought to have been negativistic in its attitude toward the historic Jew and traditional Judaism. It is a fairly widespread notion that Haskalah writers almost preached assimilation in their grandiloquent Hebrew; but that—fortunately—the Jewish masses of Eastern Europe turned a deaf ear upon that seductive yet detrimental doctrine. God be thanked, the story goes, that Jewry instinctively refused to take Haskalah ideology more seriously! It has frequently been asserted even in Hebrew criticism that the Haskalah writers urged their readers to seek their humanistic self-fulfillment outside the Jewish fold, since figures who were neither builders nor destroyers of new worlds, but mere men, who, being possessed of ordinary assets and liabilities and limited energy, unwittingly happened to be standing by some dilapidated tottering structure, so that some spectators were led to the erroneous conclusion that those 'heroes,' with Samson-like strength, took fast hold of the middle pillars upon which the house rested, bending it violently and overthrowing it." Applying this simile to Mendelssohn, Ahad Haam continues: "One of these imaginary heroes, after whom a whole century with its vicissitudes has been called, was Moses Mendelssohn— that affable, simple-hearted man, who was never ambitious nor could ever have been ambitious (in the revolutionary sense of the word), and who, if he had lived some decades earlier in Italy or in Holland, would be remembered and respected today as one of the Jewish sages, like Joseph Solomon Delmedigo or Menasseh ben Israel. Yet his time and place brought it about that, without the least intention or effort on his part, he has come to be regarded as the mainstay of all the active leaders of the period; so that the entire revolution which began in his days, and continued long after his death was named after him—the Mendelssohnian era. Thus, Mendelssohn first seemed the miraculous savior —Moses the Second, or the Third, and whatever else he was called by way of glorification; later, when the reaction to the so-called Mendelssohnian age began, Mendelssohn appeared as the Devil himself, the traitor in Jewry who brought eternal disaster upon Judaism; while, in reality, he was neither the one nor the other. He was merely a gentle, sensitive being, possessed of good sense and good taste, but weak at the time, lacking in ambition or capacity for great action, for great social reform, for wrecking the old or building the new."

But Ahad Haam's own negative attitude to much, if not most, of the modern literature created in Hebrew before his day was the result of practically the same error in judgment of which he had accused those who had read all the implications of the period of the Jewish emancipation into the personality of Moses Mendelssohn. Much of Ahad Haam's negativism in relation to Haskalah literature stemmed from his conviction, also, that Jewish self-negation in the post-Mendelssohnian decades was the result of the cringing before the non-Jewish world which Haskalah writers, in the Hebrew too, had instilled into their reading public. In fact, Ahad Haam committed the fallacy of all harsh critics of Haskalah letters before and after him when he took it for granted that Haskalah authors had preached to the Jew the philosophy which he presumably found epitomized in the well-known line by Judah Leib Gordon: "Be a Jew at home, and a human being outside." Thus, Ahad Haam also assumed that it was Haskalah literature that had engendered the well-known escapism of the emancipated Jew, his craven anxiety to disguise his Jewish identity, save, at best, when he was "at home" among his own.

Even Joseph Klausner, the historian of modern Hebrew literature, upholds this point of view to some extent. Discussing the work of Haskalah authors in Russia during the sixties and the seventies of the last century, he speaks first of the assimilationist, Jewish self-effacing tendencies of "most" Hebrew writers of those decades. "In their aspirations for Europeanism," he says, "these writers never distinguished between those values of European civilization which Jews as human beings and as members of a living people really had to adopt and those outward forms of modern civilization which undermine the socio-national forms of Jewish folk-life. . . ." Then, syllogistically,

Klausner expatiates on the corrupting influence these writers had upon their Hebrew-reading public, especially the younger generation. To quote him again: "Jewish youth were the eager disciples of their favorite [Hebrew] authors. These young people broke into the alien environment and became almost hostile to their own. Neither the Hebrew authors nor their young followers understood the universally humanistic and historically cultural significance of Judaism. . . . Most Hebrew authors in the sixties and seventies . . . did not create a Jewish affirmation in addition to that universally humanistic affirmation which demanded that their people—Jewry—should adapt itself to the conceptual world of European enlightenment." In short, Hebraic literary criticism for the past seventy years and down to our own day in Palestine, has often been inclined to read Jewish self-hate into much of the literature produced in Hebrew in the first one hundred years of the period of emancipation.

In any attempt to understand the Jewish loyalties of Haskalah literature, one fact must be stressed. With few exceptions, the Haskalah authors who wrote in Hebrew were recurrently appalled to discover that often it was the emancipated Jew who became the indifferent Jew, or even, in many cases, completely lost to Judaism and Jewishness. One most significant feature of Jewish emancipation is frequently overlooked in the evaluation of the Hebrew literature of the last two hundred years. Cultural Jewish emancipation during this period was a process engendered not by literature but by historical forces over which the literature had hardly any control. A concatenation of factors —economic, social and political—tended to bring the Jew out of the ghetto into the wide-open non-Jewish world, with certain cultural results which only coincidentally proved disastrous to historical Jewish civilization. We have already stressed the fact that the economic and social expansion of modern Jewry in one country after another regularly preceded its political emancipation. But such expansion constantly meant the cultural expansion, also, of that given Jewry. That is to say, the inevitable economic and social expansion made for the penetration of Jews into the non-Jewish cultural environment, their inevitable self-integration into the language, manners, literature and art of the country in which they happened to be. Thus, and only thus, Jews in one country after another came to desert their own tradition. They tended toward cultural assimilation, regardless of what Hebrew letters preached or did not preach.

To cite one illustration. As we have seen, politically, Prussian Jewry was emancipated in 1812. But in Berlin, the capital of Prussia, ever so many Jews were culturally assimilated in the last decades of the 18th century. Why? Because from about the middle of that century they inevitably were absorbed into the higher strata of Berlin society to which they had come to belong, first economically and then socially. The sons and daughters of the Jewish industrial and financial magnates of the capital, of Frederick the Great's *Seidenjuden, Sammetjuden* and *Münzjuden,* no longer shared with their fathers the Judaism to which the latter might still be clinging. They already spoke German or French, as did the best of the court cavaliers or members of the Huguenot population of Berlin, who constituted the earlier industrial and financial world of the Prussian capital. Like these they were inspired by Rousseau's emotional humanism, by Voltaire's iconoclastic wit, thrilled by the

ideals of liberty, equality and fraternity of French revolutionary thought. In the next decades they rounded out this
process of self-humanization by the utter denial of their
Jewishness save in some shriveled denominational sense;
or, more categorically, by conversion to Christianity.

But what had such humanistic self-fulfillment to do with
the ideology of Hebrew literature produced in Germany in
the last two decades of the 18th century? Not by the wildest
stretch of the imagination can one read into the Hebrew
writers of that period the suggestion that they had in mind
the kind of Jewish self-integration into the European civilization that finally meant large-scale conversion to Christianity or even the loss of all Jewish self-identification except
in the religious or so-called confessional sense. As a matter
of fact, sheer chronology bears out this point. The whole
period of Hebrew Haskalah in Germany is known as the
age of the *Measefim,* the literary miscellanies in which the
earliest secular Hebrew authors preached, praised and ar-
gued their new ideals in the language of the prophets, as
they loved to say. But the first *Measef* was published in
1784, that is, at least twenty to thirty years after the process
of Jewish cultural assimilation had definitely emerged in
the life of German Jewry. Furthermore, what a brief career
these miscellanies enjoyed! Established in 1784, they were
practically defunct ten years later. When in 1794 an attempt was made to revive the *Measef,* one of its stalwart
editors, Isaac Euchel, refused to share in the task because he
was certain that there was no Hebrew-reading public left
among German Jewry.

Times, people, and views—all seemed to have changed
altogether too rapidly for the promoters of Hebrew as the
language of the new humanistic Jewish civilization they had

visioned in Germany. The language of that civilization was henceforth to be German, fifteen short years after Hebrew authors had first proclaimed their conviction that it would be Hebrew. The successor of the *Measef*, indeed, is the first Jewish periodical in the German language, *Sulamith*, which appears in Leipzig in 1806. Of course, as its editors David Frankel and Joseph Wolf indicated in their programmatic articles, *Sulamith* also would continue to propagate Humanism. For Humanism, as they now declared in excellent German, was still the beautiful adornment of the new era, shedding its benefactions upon mankind. Humanism was the foundation which nurtured that most beautiful flower: the true brotherhood of man. And wherever brotherly love fills human hearts, tolerance takes the seat of honor in society. *Sulamith*, its editors promised, would aim at the propagation among the Jewish people of pure culture and humanity, the clarification of the conceptions of nature, art, and the social relations; so that Jews, too, might enjoy the blissful air of enlightenment and attain true happiness. Its humanistic ideology and its more utilitarian aim, to adjust the Jew culturally for the attainment of political emancipation, are still those of the *Measefim*. All that is missing is the Hebrew medium. But while Isaac Euchel laments the very ideals of enlightenment, since they no longer can be propagated in Hebrew, the editors of *Sulamith* take the disappearance of Hebrew as the language of Jewish humanism rather lightheartedly. They pay tribute to the *Measef* as an excellent periodical, but declare its discontinuation to have been inevitable. For the enlightened Jews of Germany, for the *hellsehende*, as the editors of *Sulamith* call them, the *Measef* is no longer indispensable: *kein notwendiges Bedürfniss*. The learned humanism as they discovered that humanistic expansion without Hebrew as the language of the soul tended to alienate the Jew from his authentic Jewish self. Yet the process of cultural emancipation repeatedly followed this pattern. Jews who became enlightened, who in country after country eagerly embraced the brave new world, soon showed the tendency everywhere to fall into the category of those whom the editors of *Sulamith* had described as no longer capable of understanding Hebrew.

Much the same process repeated itself in Galicia, Poland, Lithuania, and the Ukraine, although with marked variations from the pattern set in the last quarter of the 18th century in Germany. True enough, the disappearance of Hebrew as the intelligible medium of enlightenment was the index of a more disastrous submergence of Jewish identity in Germany than it later proved to be in Eastern Europe, with its crystallized pattern of compact Jewish living. Humanistic self-fulfillment which the individual Jew endeavored to achieve in Germany through self-integration into non-Jewish German civilization meant large-scale conversion to Christianity even in the first decades of the 19th century, or assimilation, an almost complete loss of Jewish cultural self-identification, for fully a hundred years. Among East European Jews these tendencies were far less extreme. Their deeper rootage in Jewish traditionalism, in the rich soil of a folk-life continued by millions of people for another century in itself proved a formidable obstacle to large-scale penetration of de-Judaized enlightenment. The repressive measures of the czarist government throughout the 19th century, coupled with a cruelly aggressive anti-Jewish attitude on the part of Russian Christian society, also greatly contributed to the adamantine antagonism of the Jewish masses in Russia and Poland to the ideology of cultural change advocated by Haskalah. The reiterated assertions of the Haskalah writers that the betterment of the social and economic status of the Jew depended only upon his own readiness to readjust himself culturally to the new era of human love and brotherhood could not sound too convincing to the Jewish masses in Eastern Europe.

Even the advocacy by Haskalah writers of a more equitable occupational distribution must have sounded hollow to a Jewry denied the rudimentary opportunities of daily subsistence. Galician Jews were urged by Haskalah writers to celebrate the would-be liberal edict of Joseph II of Austria in 1782, by which the Emperor sought to remove the cultural separation of the Jews from the rest of the community. Secular education and skilled manual training were opened to the Jewish population. But other provisions of this and similar statutes brought about the banishment of one-third of its numbers from the agricultural areas of Galicia and pauperized large sections of the community for generations to come. While paeans were sung by the Russian Haskalah to the charitable intentions toward Jewry of Alexander I, Nicholas I, and certainly Alexander II, the majority of Russian Jews continued to pine in the material misery of the congested Pale of Settlement. Excluded by the law of the state not only from agriculture, but from the trades and crafts as well; denied admission, except in pitifully small numbers, to the schools and universities, Russian Jews during this period must have been more than sceptical regarding the ultimate validity of the Haskalah program for a happier life.

Nevertheless, even in Russian Poland, the tendency of the few who had achieved a higher economic and social de-Judaized Humanism upon Jewish civilization was concerned. Less consciously, however, such misgivings had haunted the period all along as from time to time it checked the effect of cultural expansion upon Jewry. One hundred and twenty years ago Joseph Perl's devastating satire on Galician Jewry did not exclude the Europeanized Jews in the "enlightened" community of Brody, who already flaunted foppish culture and specious Western manners. It was not only among the hasidic rabbis that Perl failed to find a man of integrity, one whose concern was the welfare of the common people. He failed to find him also among "the intellectuals and the philosophers." The intellectuals, he mocked, resist folk-Hasidism not because of the ignorance and the superstition upon which that movement thrives, but because they hate their fellow Jews and because they oppose all that is new and revolutionary in Hasidism. Only their stupid arrogance forbids them to regard the hasidic rabbi as a truly exalted person. Indeed, the very culture of these new Jews is but sham. Their intellectual equipment is the sum total of several European novels or plays they have read, and whatever odds and ends they have picked up from lexicons and encyclopedias. At best they know how to prattle in French or Italian, and they intersperse their Jewish speech with foreign words and expressions the precise meanings of which they never know. These courageous fighters of Hasidism are frightened out of their wits in the presence of a petty government official. They are not really free thinkers, but would-be heretics, licentious and aping the non-Jew. With keener understanding of the problem, and a deeper sense of indignation, Isaac Erter depicts the crude self-seeking of such alienated Jews who "cast off the folly of their own people in order

to indulge in the folly of the Gentiles. The enlightened
Jew is never stirred by the suffering of his people. Watching the collapse of his native home, he is never moved to
prop it up; he never offers to help rid his people of its crushing ignorance, to remove the stigma which attaches to it
by raising its status. He is forever taken up with his ego
only. His frigidity is unendurable when he derides those
who cannot find peace because of the state of Jewry. With
his coldness he freezes those consumed as with fire by their
zeal in behalf of Jewry. Not at all enlightened is he! For the
love of his people does not light up the dark night of his
soul."

At best, Haskalah authors may be taken to task for one
thing only. While they frequently realized that the emancipated Jew tended to become the alienated Jew, they never
seriously stopped to consider the way out of the tragic
dilemma. They never earnestly asked themselves why Jewish self-alienation was the "norm" of Jewish emancipation. In their love for the Jew and historical Judaism they
violently demanded the revitalization of both. But they
scarcely wondered whether such revitalization was possible
so long as both the Jew and Judaism were undergoing the
process without the necessary conditions for the preservation of their historic identity.

Much earlier Hebrew writers than Ahad Haam had
realized that the whole wealth of Jewish ritual was the
historic means by which Israel had preserved its identity in
the Diaspora. Nor was Nahman Krochmal the only one
first to understand it. Most of the Haskalah writers, from
Isaac Baer Levinsohn to Peretz Smolenskin, knew it in their
hearts and frequently expressed the idea. Hence all the
blithe and blind assumptions of Haskalah ideology. Its

conscious hope and drive was the rejuvenation of the Jew
and his Jewishness. Therefore the difficulties involved in
the process, while occasionally registered and understood,
remained in the periphery of Haskalah consciousness. Of
course the Jewish religious tradition would somehow survive. Of course the Hebrew language would continue to be
the purest expression of the Jewish soul. Of course Jewish
historical identity would continue distinct and distinctive
as heretofore. These tacit assumptions could not be ex-
amined more consciously. The main objective of Haskalah
literature was digging up the precious jewel from under
the mass of rock heaped upon it in the course of the ages.
That the diamond itself was being cast away by the enlightened Jew along with the dead stones with which it had
long been covered was an embarrassing realization that
from time to time troubled the conscience of Haskalah
writers. As long, however, as there were millions of Jews
stifled by medieval conditions, those millions to be helped
ever cried for the same cure: Jewry and Judaism must wake
to a new life.

How could Haskalah literature have sensed more clearly
the inescapable dilemma involved? As was suggested in
the first chapter, the urge toward a revitalized worldly existence which Jewry has experienced in the course of the
past two hundred years has basically meant Jewry's belated
experience of the European Renaissance with its impulsions away from asceticism to a fuller life on earth. It may
be helpful to recall that in the European Renaissance those
impulsions had resulted in sharp clashes between traditional authority and the aggressively new authority of the
self-asserting human will to shape civilization in con-
sonance with man's untrammeled intellectual and emotional cravings. Fundamentally, modern Jewish history has

witnessed a similar struggle between dogmatic tradition on the one hand and the humanistic growth of the Jew on the other. Had Jewry come to experience its "Renaissance" as a people living within its own territorial bounds, the conflict between dogmatic tradition and humanistic expansion might have proved no more violent than it did in occidental society. Judaism as a religion might have seen its authority curtailed, while Jews in the more secular aspects of their civilization would still have remained Jews. As an extra-territorial people, however, Jewry was faced with more than the struggle between a religious tradition claiming full authority over human life and man's efforts to limit that authority. Jewry was faced with the question, also, of ceasing to be Jewry in everything but the religious sense. The emancipated Jew, even when he continued to regard himself as a professing Jew, inevitably tended to disappear as a member of a distinct cultural group. His culture outside of religion became the culture of the non-Jewish environment of the land in which he lived. As a professing Jew, he has tended to identify himself culturally with the native son as a German in Germany, as a Frenchman in France, as a Russian in Russia, and as an American in America. This unavoidable and tragic implication of Jewish humanistic expansion Haskalah literature surely could not have sensed too definitely in the period we have discussed. The only logical resolution of the dilemma was found by Hebrew literature in "cultural Zionism." But cultural Zionism, in its Ahad-Haamic formulation, was still in the offing even when in the late seventies of the last century Jewish social thinking had already begun to grope toward Palestinianism as the solution of the problem of the homelessness of the Jew and his Jewishness.

It is true, of course, that the Russian pogroms of 1881–

82 were the immediate cause of the earliest initiation of
Zionism, in the form of Love of Zion, as an organized
movement in Jewish life. It is equally true that the ideology
of this new movement produced in its very first years some
of the most vital and fervent social writing in contemporaneous Hebrew literature. But, for some thirty to forty
years to come, practically up to 1920, the concern with the
Zionist ideal of at least the imaginative categories of
Hebraic creativity remains rather indeterminate. The stirring effect of the pogroms of 1881–82 upon the humanistic
ideology of the Haskalah period expressed itself for the
next three or four decades in moods quite different from
indubitable gravitation toward Palestine.

The composite character of these moods in the immediate post-Haskalah years may be called one of penitence.
Hebrew writers begin to transvaluate the values of the
Haskalah period. Almost abruptly they stop haranguing
Jewry and wistfully begin to sing the deeply human worth
of the Jew and historical Judaism. They come to accept the
view that the sufferings of the Jew are not the result merely
of what Solomon Maimon had called the Jew's "reluctance
to change," and his "antagonism to sound character." The
frustration of Haskalah faith in the liberalism of the enlightened world becomes a dominant theme of Hebrew
letters. The Hebrew author who had long advocated Jewish
cultural self-liberation as prerequisite for a more liberal
treatment of the Russo-Polish Jew had been rudely jostled
out of his pet dream. No less ardent an advocate of Haskalah ideology than Judah Leib Gordon wrote in 1883 the
well-known poem "Young and old, we shall all go," in
which he urged the Jewish exodus from Russia in a mass
migration overseas. "The eternal hatred for an eternal

people," as Peretz Smolenskin phrased it, is accepted as the only basic cause of Jewish misery.

The penitent mood sensed in Hebraic letters at this juncture manifests itself above all in the revaluation of former attitudes toward ghetto-Judaism. Anticipating Ahad Haam's interpretation of Jewish ethical historicism, men like Peretz Smolenskin, Yehiel Michel Pines, Zeev Wolf Jawitz write their deeply felt and deeply thought-through evaluations of the spirituality of Judaism as a religion and of the Jew as the bearer of that spirituality. Anticipating the romanticization of the *staedtel* in all of Jewish literature, especially in the Yiddish, of the last thirty years, the poets and story writers begin to sing the piety, the simplicity, the resigned sweetness and humor of the misery of Jewish Eastern Europe, of what has recently been called "the world of Sholom Aleichem." The long-mocked obscurantists of the ghetto become its exalted "children and dreamers." The fanatical rabbi becomes the utterly selfless saint, the spiritual representative of a world that is pure learning and contemplation. The helpless, dull and cruel Melammed evolves into the ideal pedagogue whose love for children is unbounded and who transmits the eternal verities of Jewish idealism, utterly oblivious of the economic discomfort which his nagging wife naturally refuses to accept. The half-starved and ignorant shoemaker, tailor or coachman becomes the meek protagonist of a psalm-reciting religiosity. Even the shiftless, quixotic merchant evokes nothing but pathos and humor in his fruitless endeavors to eke out his livelihood by the most impossible commercial manipulations. In short, Jewish ghettoism, so long satirized in the literature, suddenly shines forth in its basic, deeply moving human worth. No wonder post-

Haskalah literature also engenders the trend that has been called neo-Hasidism. In the manner of Peretz and, later, S. Y. Agnon, Hasidism, the latest efflorescence of Jewish piety and mysticism in the history of traditional Judaism, comes into its own as a literary manner in the immediate post-Haskalah decades through men like Micah Joseph Berdichevsky, Mordecai Zeev Feierberg, and Judah Steinberg. Thus, Hebrew literature begins to vindicate itself as Jewishly loyal, as zealous in its devotion to the very Judaism which in the spirit of its humanistic drives it severely chastised during the Haskalah period. Unlike Jewish literature in a non-Jewish language, it cannot make peace with the humanistic self-fulfillment of the alienated, culturally emancipated Jew. When, therefore, the inroads made by Jewish self-alienation upon Jewish authenticity become manifest, the first reactions of this literature are in the direction of romanticism—a desperate attempt to hold on to the passing glories of waning ghetto-Jewishness by stressing its rugged worth.

The attempt, however, was desperate, historically impossible in its social implications. The exodus from the spiritual ghetto was as inevitable as the exodus from the physical ghetto. But in the course of the next few decades the old order was inexorably destined to crumble and almost to disappear. In those years some ten million East European Jews become emancipated—five million of them in the United States, the rest in Russia and elsewhere. Besides, the humanistic cravings in the heart of Jewry never cease to be deeply understood and approved of by Hebrew letters. The yearnings of the individual Jew for human expansion continue to be as important to these later decades of Hebraic creativity as they were for one hundred and fifty years before. Only the problem of preserving the Jewish identity in the sweeping rush of the Jewish individual toward worldly self-fulfillment becomes ever more pressing. It grows increasingly difficult to solve so long as the individual Jew, in greater numbers, undergoes the process of humanistic aggrandizement while the Jewish group everywhere continues to be extraterritorial. Thus the history of Jewish humanism as recorded by modern Hebrew literature evolves into its later phase—the slow groping toward Zionism.

CHAPTER IV

The Individual
and the Group

OUR PRESENT objective is to consider the peculiar relationship between Hebrew literature and the Palestinian ideal
from 1881 to about 1920. Why did Hebrew writing—more
specifically, Hebrew fiction and poetry—remain indeterminate in regard to Zionism for some thirty or forty years?
The significance of this question is first suggested by a new
development which takes place in Hebrew letters beginning
with the eighties of the last century.

Throughout the Haskalah period no hard and fast line
can be drawn between the purely literary character of Hebrew letters and their social or publicistic character. The
material and spiritual deficiencies of ghetto life so engross
the attention of all Haskalah writers that there is scarcely a
novelist or an essayist of the period, rarely even a poet, who
can afford to be the creative artist only. The Haskalah author is forever the social thinker and preacher as well. He
seldom permits himself to retreat into his individualistic
dream-world, to shut himself up with the muse in the shrine
of his ego.

This literary situation begins to change in the early eighties, and with the turn of the century the change becomes increasingly perceptible. A distinct line of demarcation is

drawn between imaginative writing and journalese. Belles-lettres, the poem and the story especially, more consciously cultivate their self-segregation from the didactic or utilitarian mood. The publicistic element is more and more eliminated from literary expression. Only the newspaper article and the more ponderous study in the literary review deal with the stirring social problems of the day. The poem, the story and the critical essay reach out for wider regions of purely creative activity.

These forty years, 1880–1920, are charged with social storm and stress. Tens of thousands of Jews, soon to become a hundred thousand a year, migrate overseas. A rising Jewish proletariat becomes increasingly class-conscious and young Jews in swelling numbers join the Russian revolutionary movements. Various new panaceas for the betterment of the political, social and economic status of the Jew in czarist Russia mushroom annually. The divine rights of Hebrew are challenged by an aggressive Yiddishism, the modernization of Jewish schools produces motley new systems of education; the viciousness of Russian anti-Semitism grows by leaps and bounds. In short, Jewish group life during these years is constantly agitated from within far more intensely, surely far more consciously, than it ever was before or during the Haskalah period. Yet Hebrew literature divorces itself more insistently from the direct treatment of social problems. These become almost exclusively the domain of the publicist. There are a few exceptions, such as Alexander Siskind Rabinowitz, who writes a novel in which he depicts the movement toward an idealistic proletarianism. Here and there, as in the verse of Isaac Kaminer, one encounters a poetical profession of socialist faith. Here and there, as in the work of Isaiah Bershadsky

or of A. A. Kabak, one finds a conscious study of the desperate effort made by some Jews to stem the tide of Russifica-
tion. The few exceptions only prove the rule. Indeed, it is
in these thirty to forty years that Hebrew letters achieve the
highest peaks of purely artistic creativity. They are the years
of Hayyim Nahman Bialik, Saul Tchernichovsky and Zalman Shneur in poetry; of Mendele Mocher Seforim, Micah
Joseph Berdichevsky and S. Y. Agnon in prose.

Strange as it may seem, Zionism also in this period seldom becomes the deliberate theme of the poet, the novelist,
or the literary essayist. And here, too, the hundred years of
Haskalah writing come to mind by way of comparison. If
one recalls the tacit zeal inherent in most Hebrew writing
during the Haskalah on behalf of the Jew and of Jewish
history at its best, it may not be hard to understand why the
dream of the land of Israel as the land of the Jewish past as
well as of his distant yet ever near future remained unconsciously real to the writing author, even during that age of
determined struggle for the humanistic growth of Jewry.
To be sure, Haskalah literature hardly ever preached the return to the land of Israel as the means of revitalizing Jewish history and psychology. Nevertheless, it rarely forgot
what it often wistfully called "all our ancient splendors,"
including Palestine: ancient Jewish independence in the
land of Israel. This is true of the entire Haskalah period,
from Moses Mendelssohn down to J. L. Gordon. Indeed,
it comes as a surprise to hear Moses Mendelssohn declare
that Jewish restoration to Palestine is one of the principles
of his religious faith: "I consider it true and certain that
the children of Abraham, Isaac and Jacob will not always
be removed from the Promised Land and scattered among
the other nations; but that God, at a time known to him
alone, will set up an anointed ruler of the House of David,

who will make this people once again a free nation, and will reign over them in the land of their fathers." Elsewhere, he speaks even more explicitly of what we call today the Jewish national revival in Palestine: "God in his mercy upon our remnant has caused it that in his law and commandments we be given a hold and a support, until the time of nuptial bliss arrives, when he will raise up the tabernacle of David from the dust, and will say to the fallen daughter of Zion: Rise upon thy feet and live! Then he will also send his spirit into our sacred language, to revive it, to put it back upon the pedestal on which it once stood." This semireligious and semifolkloristic love of Zion as the place where Israel and the history and language of Israel will some day be returned to their pristine glories; this semiconscious folk-Zionism of traditional Judaism hardly ever disappeared from the pages of Haskalah writing. For over a hundred years, it produced a variety of literary works which directly and indirectly expressed the longing for the Return.

First of all, Haskalah literature directly exploited the theme of Jewish longing for the Holy Land as well as for the resurrection of the ancient glories of Israel's past. This dual theme is the subject of a goodly amount of wistful and occasionally beautiful lyric poetry, produced long before the first glimmerings of Zionism in the eighties of the last century. It was sung by Ephraim Luzzatto (1729–1792) who belongs chronologically to an earlier age than the Haskalah period strictly so called. It was celebrated even more consciously during that period in the religio-nationalistic verse of Samuel David Luzzatto (1800–1867), in some of the good specimens of what may be called folk poetry in modern Hebrew by Meir Letteris (1800–1871), who, incidentally, translated several of Byron's *Hebrew*

Melodies; or in some of the truly great lyrics by Micah
Joseph Lebensohn (1828–1852). Nor was the lyric the
only vehicle of expression of such semiconscious love of
Zion. Suffice it to mention in this connection the numerous
historical dramas and dramatic poems written in the course
of many years. In these historic works, Hebrew authors
constantly envisioned biblical Palestine as the scene of the
action, and their vivid representations of that landscape
kindled in the hearts of their readers the yearning for the
land in which—as Micah Joseph Lebensohn wrote—"a
flower is a song, the cedar—a divine poem." Prose works,
too, kept alive the age-old yearning; some dealing with the
beauties of the Hebrew language, such as Solomon Levisohn's (1789–1821) classic study in the *ars poetica* of the
Bible; some with Palestinian as well as Near Eastern geography and Jewish history, such as the adaptations and trans-
lations by Kalman Shulman (1819–1899); or others,
novels, especially like those of Abraham Mapu, which
really may be regarded as prose-poems based upon the late
period of biblical history and inspired by a love of the land
of Israel which appears in the title of one of them: "The
Love of Zion."

Little wonder then that Haskalah literature had groped
its way toward a more conscious conception of the restoration to Palestine a considerable time before the pogroms
of 1881–1882. These pogroms initiated organized Zionism
in the form of the movements of the Love of Zion; and of
Bilu, which was the first group of young Russian Jews that
set out to do pioneering in Palestine. "Bilu" is an acrostic
formed from the first four words of a Hebrew sentence
from Isaiah: "O House of Jacob, come let us walk in the
light of the Lord." But Haskalah authors had begun much
earlier to develop ideas concerning the solution of the Jew-

ish problem in terms which were Zionist in everything but
name. Peretz Smolenskin did not embrace Zionism before
the eighties; but as early as 1868, in the programmatic editorial in which he introduced his epoch-making *Hashahar*,
he had declared that it is not at all unseemly for the modern
Jew to aspire to political independence in a Jewish state in
Palestine. About the same time, and increasingly so in the
seventies, Hebrew newspapers and periodicals devoted
their columns to the analysis of a preadumbrated Zionism,
and among those who participate in such discussions one
often finds men of letters who are only incidentally journal-
ists. Even J. L. Gordon, that severest critic of Jewish ghettoism, confesses as early as 1872 that he is not at all opposed
to the materialization of the messianic ideal, as his opponents in the arch-orthodox camp had charged. Gordon's
somewhat paradoxical confession is worth noting even today. It is not the arrival of the Messiah that he fears but the
technological unpreparedness of Jews for the restoration to
Zion. To follow the Messiah into Zion, he argues, there will
be required skilled workers and professionally trained men
—engineers, agronomists, architects, physicians and even
diplomats or statesmen. Where will the Messiah find such
a retinue of necessary technicians for the process of redemption of people and land? Surely, Gordon argues, not among
the orthodox rabbis and Yeshivah *bahurim,* whom at best
the Messiah may consult in matters of ritual. The real engineers of the Jewish restoration, therefore, the Messiah
will have to seek among the educated Jews of Western
Europe. Thus, peculiarly enough, Gordon concludes,
emancipated Western European Jews, those execrable re-
formists and apostates, are far readier than East European
orthodoxy to follow the Messiah in order to engineer Jewish resettlement in the Holy Land.

years of modern Zionism. The deep emotion of the time can hardly be detected in its poetry. It is much more evident in its sturdy publicistic articles and expository essays. Peretz Smolenskin, Yehiel Michel Pines, Moshe Leib Lilienblum, Eliezer Ben-Yehudah, and the greatest of them all, Ahad Haam, all revealed themselves as writers of vigorous intellectual prose under the stress of the pregnant idea of emergent Zionism. The poetry dedicated to the Zionist ideal was lame at its birth and continued to limp for the next forty years. Bialik and Tchernichovsky, somewhat later, almost instinctively eschewed that theme. They left the field uncontested to the Dolitzkis and the Imbers. Bialik, it is true, made his debut as a Zionist. His first published poem, *El ha-Tzippor,* was nostalgically Zionistic though not directly so. But later on he published only very little in this vein, besides the declamatory poem dedicated to the First Zionist World Congress and his well-known hymn *Tehezaknah.* Tchernichovsky's manifestly Zionist record is even less impressive in the first twenty years of his career. And what is true of these two master poets of the age is also true of others. In short, Hebrew literature seems for a good many years to have shied away from Zionism: the very theme that obviously gave it its raison d'être, its really new lease on life.

One simple reflection may help to understand this strange phenomenon. Most Hebrew writers between 1880 and 1920 undoubtedly gravitated toward Zionism, especially in its cultural aspects as presented by Ahad Haam in his essays. Yet their Zionism necessarily remained an abstract conviction rather than a living source of inspiration. It was not only that they themselves continued to live in the Diaspora, in Russia and Poland as well as in Western Europe, particularly in Germany and Switzerland; it was not only that they lacked the tangible inspiration of the Palestinian soil and air, or that their sensory world—the most essential element of imaginative writing—remained the Swiss, the German, or the Russian scene. Their Zionism was at best only a poignant abstraction because they did not see before them a Jewry that was sufficiently aroused to make the Palestinian dream a reality. Except for a small trickle of young idealists to the land of Israel, good Zionists the world over continued to live the world over. Thus Zionism was with the Hebrew writer of the period only a hesitant new faith in the light of which he could, perhaps, sense more deeply the tragedy of the conscious Jew not yet geared to saving his Jewishness in the only way possible: by settling in the land of Israel. Indeed, the cruel probing of the new Jew who refuses to live his Zionism in the flesh becomes the function of Hebrew literature in this period of widespread theoretical Zionism.

Theoretically, indeed, Hebrew literature at the turn of the century has already embraced Zionism. Abstractly, it regards Zionism as the only sound method by which the Jew may achieve his humanistic growth while at the same time preserving his Jewishness. With very few exceptions, Hebrew authors henceforth fully subscribe to Ahad Haam's teachings. They are aware of the place of Judaism as an authentic spiritual force in human history; and convinced that only if restored to Palestine in sufficiently large numbers to constitute, eventually, a majority of the population, can the Jewish people as a culturally autonomous community again begin to weave the golden thread of its creative genius. With Ahad Haam the Hebrew writer now generally glories in the Jewish past; with Ahad Haam he believes that historical Judaism has made its magnificent imprint upon world civilization. Like Ahad Haam, he refuses to call it the "Jewish mission," for he feels somewhat embarrassed by a term that suggests something divinely preordained. But, like Ahad Haam again, the Hebrew writer believes that it is impossible "to dedicate Jewry to spiritual missions or historic goals as long as the Jewish people has not attained the natural physical goal of every living organism; has not created for itself living conditions which fit its spiritual character, and which will permit it to develop its forces and capacities, its own specific form. For only when it has attained all this will it be possible for the process of its life, in course of time, to draw Jewry to the function for which it may prove itself best suited—that of 'teacher' of others, and once again, in terms of the modern age, may be of universal use to all mankind. Should then," Ahad Haam concludes, "philosophers arise among us who declare that the function of our people is the mission for which it was formed, I may not, indeed, be able to share that belief, but I shall not quarrel about a difference in terminology only. . . ."

Whatever terminology is used to describe the historical function of Judaism, the Hebrew writer of this period accepts it as his own in the spirit of Ahad Haam's teaching. Judaism has played an important role in the evolution of human civilization, Judaism can and must go on playing its historic part. All that is needed is a new framework suitable for its continued functioning as a universally significant force. Such a framework, the writer knows, is no longer provided by the spiritual ghetto of former days. He observes the ghetto crumbling right before his eyes under the furious onrush of the tide of cultural emancipation.

Once out of the ghetto the individual Jew—numbering millions—inevitably comes to steep himself in the national
civilization of the country in which he lives—in language
and in psychology, in ethos and mythos, in everything save,
at best, a greater or lesser measure of religious self-identification. Thus, it is not a question of negating Diaspora-
Judaism. Judaism in the Diaspora negates itself. Again, as
Ahad Haam expresses it: "Our forefathers, it is true, lived
their national life on foreign soil. But they achieved such
extraterritorial national existence only by shutting themselves off entirely from the life of the rest of humanity;
while we—today—no longer can live such a segregated
life, removed from universal civilization. . . . How, then,"
he asks, "can these two contradictions be reconciled: on the
one hand, full participation in the life of culture which in
every country manifests itself in the national form of the
dominant people; and on the other hand, the full development of a specifically Jewish national life that is forever
suspended in mid-air, with nothing firm to support it?" Of
necessity, therefore, Hebraic writing accepts Ahad Haam's
cultural Zionism which he states in these words: "It is our
privilege also to become a majority in one land under the
heavens, a land where our historical right is indubitable, re-
quiring no farfetched proof, and in whose historic atmosphere our truly national existence may develop in keeping
with our genius, without shrinking and confining itself only
to certain limited functions. Only then may the rest of our
people, although scattered in all countries, hope that our
national center will imbue them with its spirit, and will
give them the strength to live through its life, even though
they may be deprived of their national rights wherever they
are."

Yet this fully formulated conception of the only way in which the Jewish historical identity may be preserved in full remains only a passive awareness in the Hebrew literature of the period. It does not preach or sing the return to Zion as the only cure for what Ahad Haam calls "the tragedy of Judaism" in the modern world. Only the tragedy is sung or lamented. The cure for it hardly ever becomes the direct theme of poem or story. The breakdown of the ghetto walls, most vividly depicted in the imaginative writings of these years, points only indirectly the way to the land of Israel, never urging it upon those fleeing from within the fallen ghetto walls. The psychological story and beautifully molded poem of the period ultimately led to Palestine; but this result was unintentional, for Zionism was never their manifest theme.

In the late nineties, Mordecai Zeev Feierberg wrote a novelette entitled "Whither?" Inferior from an artistic point of view, this story sets the tone of much of Hebrew fiction in the period we are analyzing. Nahman, the youthful hero of the story, is the protagonist of the young Jewry of several decades to come who recurrently ask the question: "Whither?" Raised in the home of a pious, mystically inclined father, Nahman in early childhood absorbs all the influences of melancholy yet stirring ghetto Jewishness: the age-old tales of suffering, the inspiring legends of saints and martyrs. His whole world is the arena in which good and evil, God and Satan, wage eternal warfare. That world looks to man for its ultimate redemption. Man, meaning of course no one but the Jew, must fight evil in order to redeem the Divine Spirit itself from its imprisonment in corrupt matter. The lesson Nahman is taught by his father is always the same: he, the Jewish boy, must become God's own sol-

dier, surrendering his whole being for the sake of a world
that must be led out of earthly darkness to heavenly light.
But as he grows up Nahman is tempted. As he stoops over a
volume of the Talmud, the young lad begins to feel the ineffable beauties of sky and water, of the twitter of a bird
flying by the open window, of the lush moistness of sprout-
ing grass. A new longing stirs in his heart—"a longing
just to look quietly, without thinking, to look for hours on
end, at the blue clouds, and drink in with the perfect glad-
ness of serene childhood the varied wonderful sounds that
fill space." It is then that the volume of the Talmud suddenly appears so very dreary to Nahman, and the synagogue
where he studies so unbearably sad. The synagogue and the
Talmud seem deathlike, while the dancing sunbeams in
the window beckon with irresistible life. It is then that the
young lad's life registers its first inner tear. The only conscious feeling is, "One must get out of here—but one step
out, and there is life." Indeed, the step is taken, but it does
not lead the young man into the glorious non-Jewish world
where it once seemed to lead so many heroes of Haskalah
fiction. Young Nahman certainly evolves into the small-
town heretic. He studies science and philosophy. He even
blows out a candle one Yom Kippur night, "before the eyes
of all Israel," in Feierberg's words. But whatever such
apostasy means to the congregation, to the young man, in
his own thoughts, his sinful act is the symbol of the stifled
cry in his heart: "Blow out the light of the Galut—a new
candle must be lit!" Yet Nahman never finds his way to
lighting that "new candle" in Jewish history. Even as he is
lost in his personal life, so he remains forlorn all his living
days as a Jew. He loves and then marries. But the dear eyes
of his young wife frighten him with their very love. He

knows that he belongs to a dying civilization which is so
precious that his impulse is to leave home and his loved
young wife and give all he possesses to his people. Even the
beautiful world outside the small town, which looks "like
a veritable graveyard," offers no place of refuge. The wide-
open world, beautiful as it is, is to Nahman the alien West
—the West that he knows to be "the inexorable enemy of
Jewry and Judaism." Where, then, is he to go? The only
answer is that of Zionism—Eastward. Yet Nahman himself
never gets there. He inevitably accepts the verdict long pro-
nounced by his fellow townsmen that he is "mad," literally
mad. He himself declares toward the end of the story: "I
have gone mad, because I never knew whithersoever I
should turn. Now let a new and living generation arise and
go before the people."

That Palestinian-minded generation had not yet arrived;
only a handful symbolic of the possibilities of a newly re-
generated Jewry had emerged at the turn of the century.
Young Jews in their tens and hundreds of thousands had
indeed discovered that it was but one step out of the synagogue—and there was life. They were all fleeing from the
synagogue as from a death-house, but not eastward. They
were rushing, in turbulent tides, toward the alien West: to
Western Europe, and farther on, overseas to America. Hebrew fiction, therefore, for two or three decades knows only
the story of the "uprooted." The "uprooted" becomes a
standard epithet for those fugitives from Judaism who
hardly ever arrive in the spiritual sense. They are the young
Jews who come to the metropoles of the world, seeking forgetfulness of the gravelike home town. Yet they discover
that they cannot forget it. The father's prayer shawl and
the mother's Sabbath candles are memories which block the

true enjoyment of Western music and art—a music engendered in the shadows of the cathedral, an art nurtured by the symbolism of the crucifix. The seductive beauties of Western literature are often dimmed by unexpectedly intruding echoes of the synagogal sounds, of the reading of the Torah and the wistful intoning of talmudic texts. The allurements of the coldly beautiful daughters of the Gentiles are beclouded by early childhood fears of the steely scorn in the blue eyes of the *goy*. These fugitives from the ghetto therefore forever remain in a kind of no man's land, in what Berdichevsky called "between the walls" of two eternally segregated worlds. They are seldom guided to Feierberg's East by Hebrew fiction, which vividly portrays only the horror of the vacuum created by the escape from the ghetto. For some Jews that horror could not be exorcised by card playing or carousing, nor by joining intellectual circles holding forth on the greatness of art and philosophy, or vociferating on the salvation of man through socialism and, later, communism. Some such were impelled toward Palestine as the only way to normalize their personal lives as well as to revitalize Jewish civilization. But as long as the flight from the ghetto was directed westward rather than eastward, Hebrew fiction, also, could do no better than trace the tragic implications of that flight for the soul of the individual Jew.

The same is true of the great poetry of those years. To take the most striking illustration: Bialik is known as the poet of the National Renaissance. But few people seem to realize that he was not crowned with that title for celebrating the glories of Zion and the greater glories of those who took it upon themselves to "caress the dust of our land," to fertilize it with their tears and blood into the rich sod from which a rejuvenated Judaism must spring forth some day. In his own day, and even more so later on, Bialik guided thousands of Jews to Palestinian pioneering by singing the heartbreaking tragedy of the glory that was synagogal Judaism, rather than by writing paeans to the new Judaism yet unborn. Bialik, of course, was the singer of spiritual Judaism whose like Jewish literature had not known since the days of Judah ha-Levi. But the setting in which he visualized those Judaistic splendors was the synagogue in which the bereaved Shekhinah was completely bereaved. The Shekhinah already sheltered him under her broken wing when from time to time he peered orphanlike into the emptiness of a synagogue that but now had throbbed with traditional Jewish thought and feeling. The setting for his glorification of the eternal Jewish spirit was the sorrowful vacuousness of the Yeshivah from which he and thousands of his fellows had already fled and were fleeing to the shrines of new and alien gods. If Bialik inspired some of those fugitives to return to the fold by setting out to till the new soil of Jewish continuity in Palestine, it was not because he painted for them the beauties of Sharon and Carmel, as had done, however ineptly, some of the second-rate poets. Whether beautiful or not, Sharon and Carmel as the haven of refuge for crumbling historical Judaism suggested themselves to some readers of Bialik only because they felt more deeply than their fellows the pain of the bereaved Shekhinah, of the godliness of Israel forsaken in the headlong rush of Jews out of the ghetto.

Moreover, the poetry of those years had also fathomed the meaning of the tragedy of the homeless and persecuted Jews as fully as that tragedy was understood by the fathers of so-called political Zionism, such as Leon Pinsker and

Theodor Herzl. The ominous hatred of the Jew which threatened Jewish existence physically produced some of the most masterful timely verse in modern Hebrew as well as some of its finest historical poems and ballads. It was in 1904—forty years before the destruction of six million Jews —that Bialik had cried out in the name of world Jewry, "To me the whole earth is one gallows!" Two years earlier a harmonious soul like Tchernichovsky, the most truly universal poet Hebrew literature has produced, depicted in the figure of a medieval Jew, a victim of the Crusades, the madness, to which the bloody fury of Gentile hatred may drive the sanest and the most humane son of Israel. Conversely, Bialik, Tchernichovsky, Jacob Cohen and Zalman Shneur, repeatedly in those years portrayed heroic scenes and individual Jewish heroes by way of driving home the meaning of Jewish historical tenacity. Jewish physical heroism throughout the ages is one of the glorious subjects of the poetry of this period, which inspired much of the epic character of the Palestinian upbuilding of our age, known as Halutziut. Yet that heroic singing, too, did not stress the moral of the song. It seldom, if at all, explicitly called upon young Jews to emulate the heroism of their forebears by setting out to Eretz Israel where such martyrdom could find the necessary conditions for its creative expression in this day and age. In fact, heroic Jewish history seems to have inspired the poetry of the period mainly because the poets looked in vain for Jews capable of living the only heroic life for them at that time—life in Palestine. It was only some twenty-five years later that Bialik discovered his "dead of the wilderness" resurrected in pioneering Eretz Israel. Only then did he declare himself "mere dust" for the feet of Palestinian pioneers to tread upon. Berdichevsky, too, for

It is rebellion, the rebellion of historically suppressed individualism. It is, also, and above all, a never-ending straining to break the shackles by which traditional Judaism has fettered the individual Jew from time immemorial. His opponents, including Ahad Haam, identified his rebellious individualism with Nietzscheanism. Indeed, more than any of his contemporaries in Hebrew letters he forever knocked at the gates of eternity, seeking to lift the veil from cosmic existence, to understand the ultimately glorious meaning of being and non-being. In everything he wrote, one senses the endless yearning for the complete life, for the emergence of the original masterful personality; "Man is the eye of the universe," he declares. "Man's will is the God of the universe; the will of the individual is king of all propensities, the sum total of all potentialities." But whether or not he was Nietzschean, his was the full-throated cry for Jewish individualism, for the untrammeled self-expression of the Jewish soul which it had been denied by historical Judaism.

Little wonder, then, that of all post-Haskalah writers he alone had only admiration for the humanistic revolt of the Hebrew Haskalah writers. "With the Haskalah, with the age of criticism," he wrote, "there appeared among us the first buds of freedom; we were granted the freedom to examine thoughts, opinions and actions. From theologians, from guardians of an antiquated theology, we were changed into men who observe and examine, who ask and enquire. . . . The best Maskilim were people whose hearts went out to their suffocating, imprisoned fellow Jews, who felt the strangulation and the grief of countless generations . . . the best Maskilim remonstrated with their forefathers, held them to account for the misery of their descendants. . . . We are an ancient people, submerged by a heritage that is altogether too rich, by a deluge of thoughts, feelings and values transmitted to us, so that we no longer can live in our pristine simplicity, just being, essentially being. Our egos are not our own, our dreams and our thoughts are not our own, our will is not the one implanted in us: everything we were taught long ago, everything, has been handed down to us. Everything is defined and designated within set limits and boundaries, measured and weighed, ruled and legislated; so that those among us who crave to know themselves are forlorn . . . they never can find their own ego." Naturally, therefore, Berdichevsky's sympathies go out to all the skeptics, heretics and rebels in Jewish history who were, like himself, denied the freedom of questioning the collective values of Israel and the law of Israel. He is with the false prophets, with the kings and the heroes subdued by the rigorous true prophets of biblical times in the name of God's will. He is with the Hellenizing Jews and the Sadducees of the Second Commonwealth. He is with the apostate Elisha ben Abuyah and with Bar Kokhba. He is with Spinoza and Uriel Acosta—in short with all the apocryphal writers and writings, with all the rejected and banned men, movements and writings in Israel, down to the Hasidim and the Haskalah. Of course, his heart bleeds as he looks upon modern Jewry. For he, too, sees the terrifying disintegration of Jewish life in which the breakdown of the ghetto walls has resulted. "We are torn to pieces. The one extreme forsakes the House of Israel and moves on to the alien world, offers up to it the creativeness of its soul and spirit, and gives up to it its best energies; the other extreme, the pious group, still dwells in its dark alleys, observing and keeping what it has been commanded. The enlightened ones, those who steer the middle course, are their interpretations of historical Jewry and Judaism, may have had more in common than either believed, insofar as their vision of a resurrected Israel was concerned. It is a point worth noting that Ahad Haam had laid his finger on the "tragedy of Judaism" affecting Jewry as a historical group. Jewry as a historical group, he insisted, could not continue creatively unless its collective will to live were resurrected. Once the Jewish will to continue began to register consciously, he assumed, Jewry would naturally tend, in part at least, to transplant itself to the land of Israel where its historical functioning would be normally resumed. Berdichevsky, on the other hand, spoke on behalf of the Jewish individual who, in his own person, represented both the tragedy of a historic order that had passed and an anguished diffidence toward the new order emerging. It was that anguish of the ailing modern Jew that Berdichevsky depicted without pretending to reassure him in the least. Thus, in the main Berdichevsky too represented the social psychology of the Hebrew literature of the period. Group Judaism could not find the solution of its problem even in the land of Israel, unless individual Jewishness no longer meant the suppression of the humanized individual by that very group Judaism against which he had revolted. The social aims of the literature were destined to be at least partially realized in present-day Israel. It is in the last thirty years that modern Jewish history has come to find in Palestine the only place in the world where historic Judaism and humanistic culture are approaching a satisfactory reconciliation. The effect of the beginnings of this reconciliation upon Hebrew writers has marked truly new directions in Hebrew letters.

In our attempt, then, to understand whatever is new in

Palestinian literature, we must bear in mind one thing above all. The new spirit has been breathed into it by the appearance of that type of Jew of whose emergence Hebrew literature had despaired up to 1920. That new Jew has been, and still is, the main source of Palestinian literary inspiration. It may not be a digression to point out that in the annals of Zionism itself that new Jew, the Halutz, has proved the great phenomenon which has saved Zionism from degenerating into another pseudo-messianic chapter in Jewish history. Turning for a moment from our literary inquiry to the history of Zionism, we must pause to recall the hopelessness with which Zionist ideology was faced thirty or forty years ago; that is, even after it had been fully formulated by Herzl, on the one hand, and by Ahad Haam, on the other.

That hopelessness may best be illustrated by a few quotations from a well-known document in the history of Labor Zionism, generally referred to as the "Vitkin Manifesto." That stirring call which in 1906 Joseph Vitkin sent forth from Palestine to Jewish youth in the Diaspora reads in part as follows: "The major causes of our blundering lie in our search for a short cut, our belief that the attainment of our goal is close at hand. In this belief, we have built castles in the air. In our imagination we have seen ourselves flying straight to the goal, practically without effort or sacrifice on our part . . . and so we have turned with contempt from the harder road which is perhaps the surest, and in the end, the shortest. . . . Indeed, brothers, our strength is limited, though our purpose is high. For that very reason do not let us sit with our arms folded, if we still register the will to live. Rather, for the selfsame reason, we must exert all our energies, and devote ourselves with unbounded love, with unstinted self-sacrifice, and endless patience. . . . We must work and struggle to redeem our land, and fight with the courage of those for whom there is no possible retreat; with a fury equal to that of animals robbed of their young. . . . God forbid that we deceive ourselves, or the people whose cause we would champion, by describing the task as easy, the road as short. . . . Let us be fully aware that our ships are burned, that for us there is no other way in the whole world. We must train and educate ourselves to face this fact squarely, and in this spirit we must educate our coming generations. . . . Know, brothers, your people is sick and unhappy. Expect from it no help, encouragement or reward. Do not come to it with complaints or demands. Come rather to help and to awaken, and your greatest, your highest reward will be the realization of the vision itself. Hasten and come. . . . For yet a while longer, and we here . . . alone . . . shall perish."

It is not for us to inquire here how a Vitkin or his lonely fellow pioneers in the Palestine of the early years of this century could possibly have believed that there were such individuals still left in Israel, in the midst of rushing headlong into Ezekiel's "wilderness of the nations," into the no man's land of would-be emancipation. That the Hebrew writers of the period hardly believed that such Jews existed is amply proved by the poetry of Bialik and the prose of Berdichevsky. Their existence was more than doubted even by Joseph Hayyim Brenner, who lived in Palestine from 1908 until his truly saintly death in 1921, in one of the first Arab riots in the country. As late as the end of 1919—two years after the Balfour Declaration—the anguished Zionist in him could at best produce a Jewish defiance of all logical despair—his now famous phrase "in spite of it all." "In the psychology of young Jews throughout the Diaspora," he wrote in 1919, "there must emerge a sense of 'in spite of it all.' That 'in spite of it all,' which must always come at the end of all negative calculations. In spite of it all! The more especially so, since in Eastern Europe the future is very gray, and the present very dark; since there is nothing to lose, and urgency calls that we do start from the very beginning, happen what may. Only that pioneer in whom the 'in spite of it all' has become part and parcel of his being, the Halutz who is prepared for everything, not in words alone—he may come here, he and no other."

Brenner's writing, indeed, proved the electrical storm in the life of his generation. His capacities of human love verged on the angelic; but there was something of the black angel about him too. Each stir of his wings sent a shudder through the flesh. Yet that every shudder kindled the fire of revolt. A word of complacency, a phrase of self-blinding smugness was anathema to him. If he never allowed himself the comfort of self-deception, he offered no illusory peace of mind to others either. If in his own eyes he was eternally the Dostoevskian sinner, always the penitent, conscious of his own frailties, he roused others also to look deeply into their hearts. All human pain throbbed in his soul, and he yearned always for the pure and wholesome life. Strangely enough, his very despair called his readers to a life that was truly creative. His self-searching for the discovery of the Jew in him was a fructifying factor in the lives of many forlorn Jews of the first two decades of this century. Yet, even he, who lived in the land of Israel where he saw germinal of Halutziut with his own eyes, greatly doubted whether the seeds of the Palestinian revival promised true fruition. In short, only some thirty years ago, Hebrew literature little dreamed that the new Jew it had visioned for over one hundred and fifty years was coming into being. It still hesitated to recognize the beginnings of the synthesis of historic Jewish identity and the expanded human personality in the character of the Halutz, of the culturally emancipated Jew inwardly coerced to link his individualistic yearnings to the struggle of his people for self-preservation.

CHAPTER V

Halutziut
in Palestinian Literature

PALESTINE literature reacts with a new life to the great unprecedented experience of Jewish self-rehabilitation in the
historic homeland. New perspectives, new moods and attitudes manifest themselves. The whole tone has a new ring,
a verve and vigor different from anything to be found in
the preceding periods of the mother-literature.

The problem of Jewish survival, which for several decades at least has been an essential element in whatever there
is of social significance in modern Hebrew letters, is still a
basic issue confronting Palestinian literature, burdened as
it is with social-mindedness, perturbed as it is by social
anxieties as few contemporary literatures are.

Social significance is a term which today scarcely requires
elucidation. It has been in the forefront of literary criticism for the last twenty years, and its implications are only
too obvious even to the layman. Literature, it has been ar-
gued and taught, can no longer remain a merely descriptive
or even interpretative art. It cannot go on merely mirroring
life; it must become an art which molds life. It must guide
society rather than merely portray human relations, even
against a social background which it tacitly criticizes. Im-
plied criticism, subordinate to the objective requirements

of literary art, must, it would seem, make room for the explicit annunciation of the arrival of the new—the "ideal"
—values toward which society gropes.

However tenable or untenable such a philosophy of literature may be theoretically, it seems to have been inherent
in most of modern Hebrew writing. From its halting beginnings in the 18th century to its latest full-throated utter-
ances in Palestine, Hebrew literature has been intimately
connected with all the vital manifestations of Jewish group
living, furthering some of them passionately, but often
even violently challenging some and bitterly condemning
others. More significant still, it has always pioneered among
those forces that have impelled and channeled the Jewish
group will, calling the group to new forms of living, setting
up new standards, anticipating social ideals long before
they crystallized into organized movements, creeds and
parties.

Hebrew literature has always been social-minded. It has
even been revolutionary in some of its conceptions. Yet it
is easy to overemphasize its revolutionary character, which
is far more modest than connotations of class struggle
might suggest.

It is not because socialism has been preached very effec-
tively in modern Hebrew that one can speak of the social
significance of the literature. Indeed, some of the first attempts to propagate socialism in the Jewish ghettos of Eastern Europe, in the latter half of the 19th century, were made
in Hebrew. Even cosmopolitanism, the dream to which
ever so many young Jewish radicals are still addicted, the
dream of a day when all peoples and nationalities will
simply become humanity, found its earliest expression in
the Jewish ghetto in the language of the Bible and the Rab-

bis. Needless to say, various "isms" of radical social doctrine have in recent years been preached in good Hebrew in
Israel. And the social outlook of modern Hebrew literature
has always been reflected in its continued preoccupation
with the social and economic advancement of the Jewish
masses. But the most markedly social characteristic of modern Hebrew writing and the one that is truly revolutionary
to this day has been its intense realization of the almost
superhuman transformation required of the individual
Jew, in order to make possible the no less tremendous transformation of a disintegrating Jewish people into a normally
functioning community even in a land of its own.

Essentially, the central social problem of Hebrew literature may be formulated very simply: How can the Jewish
people be saved as a people in a world struggling toward a
new and better social and economic order? While as part
of human society we share with the rest of humanity the
turmoil of this period of social transition, how can we in-
sure our survival as a people not only during this time of
world-wide travail, but also in that coveted ideal state of a
well ordered society to which we aspire with the rest of
mankind?

Thus, the social significance of Hebrew literature does
not possess the glamor of a universal doctrine; but its revolutionary character, paradoxically enough, lies precisely in
its stubborn refusal to identify the Jewish question with
the social struggles of universal man. While it recognizes
that Jewish history is an integral part of human history,
Hebrew literature does not regard the anomalies of Jewish
life in the modern world as mere symptoms of the general
maladjustments of human society; and consequently it does
not see the cure of the anomalies as wholly dependent upon

the cure of general social ills. Rightly interpreted, therefore, the revolutionary character of modern Hebrew literature is to be found in its tireless insistence first of all upon our will to survive as a people even in the most ideal world-order to be achieved by mankind; and conversely, upon the impossibility of such survival, even in the most conceivable ideal state of human society, unless we ourselves normalize our group existence; by acquiring those characteristics of healthy group living of which we are deprived by the extra-territorial nature of our people. It is specifically since its emergence from the ghetto, during a century and a half of actual or nominal emancipation, that Jewry has tended to become more disintegrated, more characterless than ever before in its long history. And while it has constantly re-affirmed the will of the Jewish people to persist, Hebrew literature has been calling upon Jewry to face squarely its own extinction unless it measures up to the formidable task of re-establishing itself as a normally functioning national organism.

Elementary as these two assertions appear, they constitute to this day the most provoking challenge to all that is weak and cowardly in Jewish life. Not a few among us, perhaps, are ready to assert today the Jewish will to survive as a people; but not many of us are ready to admit that our life as a people is doomed unless we ourselves restore it to normal health. No wonder, then, that both the emotional and intellectual stress of Hebrew literature is largely to be found in the assertion of these principles of a new Jewish creed. No wonder that this theme pervades every form of Hebrew writing—not only the purely speculative or even semiphilosophical order, but also, fiction, poetry and essay, and, to some extent, the drama.

Indeed, taken in its entirety, Hebrew literature does not simply preach survival. It literally cries out for survival. It does not advocate or argue; it utters in a thousand different voices the solemn warning that our life, our historicity, is threatened with extinction unless we as a group return to those forms of healthy group living which alone can give us a new lease on life. Whatever greatness may be found in Hebrew poetry or fiction does not derive from jingoistic swashbuckling; nor does it even manifest a self-complacent certainty of our survival as a people. Quite the contrary, it is due to a profoundly tragic realization of our utterly weak and decentralized will, the infirmity of our purpose, to bring about our own regeneration. H. N. Bialik, the poet of the Jewish Renaissance, is the surgeon who most cruelly dissects the soul of the modern Jew who finds his salvation in lip service, homage paid to nationalistic slogans and hymns, while remaining blind to the abyss that gapes beneath his feet. M. J. Berdichevsky and J. H. Brenner, in novel, story and essay, lash this tendency of even political and cultural Zionists to intoxicate themselves with fantastic dreams of the almost miraculous salvation of the Jewish people promised by political Zionism. Zionism, as it appears in Hebrew literature, rather means facing the cold excruciating fact that the restoration of the land to the people is the painfully slow process of the people returning to the land, of individual Jews shouldering the task of returning as individuals, each settling in the land himself, each undergoing the metamorphosis of the returning exile.

And conversely, Hebrew literature maintains that not by submerging of the Jewish strain in other cultures, but only by rediscovering its own genius through the return to the land of Israel, can the Jewish people once again come to make its authentically Jewish contribution to human civilization. But, here again, the best in Hebraic expression is quite "revolutionary" in the challenge it holds out, not only to the mentality of the Jew as such, but also to the fondest dreams of Zionism. As sung in Hebrew letters, the "cultural return" means first of all the capacity of individual Jews to undertake the task, the wholehearted will of such individuals to change their own lives in "the land of the fathers" and thereby—thereby only—bring about the regeneration of the people. Only through a poignantly realistic perception of the part to be played in this process by the individual absorbing the land of Israel into his individual psyche does Hebrew literature envisage the Jewish collectivity as striking its roots into the soil of Palestine and rediscovering the way to revitalization of Jewish civilization. Only through a clear vision of the revitalization of the Jewish psychology in an individualistic sense does Hebrew literature allow itself to dream of the day when a revitalized Jewish civilization may once again enrich civilization.

In its great lyric poetry, in novel and short story as well, the individual Jew yearns for his human redemption, for his intellectual and emotional aggrandizement—a Renaissance all his own. Rarely does he forget the tragedy of his Jewish history, past and, especially, present. And in his intense concern for his own destiny, he feels an inner compulsion to link his longings to those of his people. Hebrew literature inevitably identifies the individual with the group as it questions the fate of both. For fate is only character, as Goethe once observed.

The new and resonant note introduced into Hebrew literature by the Palestinian experience emanates not so much, perhaps, from enthusiasm over the actual achievements of

Zionism in the land of Israel, remarkable as those have been, but from a deep sense of wonder at the way in which they alone have made possible the spiritual rebirth of Jewish youth which has resulted in a pioneering spirit unknown for two thousand years of Jewish history—Halutziut.

For Halutziut is the complete self-identification of the individual Jewish pioneer with the group will of Jewry to rehabilitate itself historically in its ancient homeland. And, for sixty years, beginning with the vaguely sentimental nostalgia in the poetry of the Love of Zion period to the clear and often strident voices of contemporary Israel, Hebrew poets have been constantly aware that the ideal of the "return" would be realized only if enough Jews should become convinced not only that the Jewish people must return to its land for its own survival, but also, that for themselves, in the strictly personal sense, living and working in Palestine was the be-all of existence. The actual fruition of this hope struck Palestinian literature with a breath-taking impact. The dazzling experience, not yet fully assimilated, has tended to produce more rhapsodical poetry than mature, seasoned prose.

M. J. Berdichevsky was ready to accept Zionism, if only, as he put it, he could really see young Jews ready to leave for Palestine and settle there as unassuming workers rather than continue to dream of Zion and long for it from afar. J. H. Brenner never ceased to vibrate between his great hope for Jewry, bolstered as it was by his closeness to the handful of pioneers he found in Palestine, and his fears that those few hundred Halutzim were the "last of the Mohicans" of Jewish history. Contemporary Israeli literature has recorded the swelling of that small band into a vast army, and is still staggered by the wonder of it. For it evalu-

ates the greatness of Halutziut not so much by the actual
achievements of the pioneers, great as these are, as by the
phenomenal metamorphosis which thousands upon
thousands of young Jews have undergone the world over
before they could become that army of pioneers. Of course,
the colonizational development of Palestine in and for itself is a phenomenal reality which has struck a resounding
chord in Palestinian poetry and prose. But as appraised by
this literature the marvels of Eretz Israel's reality: one million Jews settled in the land within the past thirty years,
many hundreds of new agricultural settlements established,
populous cities and towns teeming with industrial and cultural activities—in short, all the assets of a revitalized
Israel as it faces the world today—are but indexes of the
inner growth of the Jewish people to an ideal which has
come of age as the most humanizing force in modern Jewish history.

The most articulate self-assertion of the literature as
Palestinian, as indigenous to the soil of the new land of
Israel, defines itself, above all, in terms of a new type of Jew
emerging. This authentically new voice is the voice of
the Halutz, the young Jew who has become deeply ashamed
of his over-intellectualized, over-spiritualized, over-volatile
self on the college campus, in the metropolitan café, or in
the parlor of a semi-affluent home, where he holds forth on
the grandest schemes for rebuilding the world, for produc-
tivizing society and collectivizing human wealth, while he
himself, self-pampered and as often as not incapable of
earning his daily bread by physical labor, has recourse to
nothing but words. As sensed by the literature of contemporary Palestine, Halutziut, in its creative fervor and pain, is
a kind of penance done by Jewish history, by Jewish psy-

chology, at once both collective and individual. In many respects the literary self-expression of the land of Israel, in the novel and short story above all, is a direct continuation of modern Hebrew literature which for several decades has mirrored the vicissitudes of Jewish psychology as it struggles with itself and against itself. But the victorious issue of that struggle, Halutziut, is the new theme introduced into Hebrew letters by their Palestinian phase.

Few, if any, of the creative writers in Palestine are consciously tendentious either in choice of theme or in treatment. In fact, the Palestinian reading public frequently cries out against what it regards as the detachment of its Hebrew authors, their deliberate refusal to respond artistically to the all-too-many agitations, national, political and social, which imbue the local atmosphere with a febrile quality, ever-present in effect and always changeable as to cause. Literary critics, also, especially in the many different party journals, frequently register similar complaints. The reasons for this situation are obvious. Jewish life in Palestine is so charged with social excitation that its literature barely seems to keep pace with the incessant intensity, with the creative throb manifesting itself in endless triumphs over endless trials and tribulations. The Palestinian author is often expected by his public to react to the daily recurrences of the community life almost as immediately and directly as does the journalist in his daily column or editorial. Fortunately however for literary values, the poets and prose writers of the country respond to these stimulations more slowly and also more subtly. Actually, the social element is rarely absent from their work. Yet by the alchemy of art this element is blended with so many others into a realm of existence at once so like reality and so unlike it, that its strictly Palestinian, or even Jewish, character may not be sufficiently obvious to a reading public intent upon self-discovery in the neo-Jewish, or Palestinian, sense.

For Palestinian literature is fundamentally universalistic, concerned with the human in the Jew—even in the Palestinian Jew—rather than with the specifically Judaic alone. Of course, as in any national literature, both elements, the purely ethnic and the more universally human, are intertwined too intricately to be dissociated even in the mind and heart of Palestinian authorship. Emphasis on the will-to-be of the group does not obliterate the physiognomy of the individual in the lyric poetry which, naturally enough, still gravitates toward the everlasting preoccupations of the poet's soul with itself and the multifarious world in which it seeks to find its bearings; with the poet's relations to the eternal fixtures of the lyric art: God, Nature and Man. Palestinian fiction, too, necessarily concentrates upon individual psychology, upon the attempts of individual men and women to orient themselves in the world, not only as Jews but as human beings. In general, such attempts at self-orientation are unusually complicated for characters in Jewish fiction and in the Hebraic particularly, because as Jews they are beset with perplexities unknown to any other species of man. But the purely human element is never lost sight of even when the background is the traditional Jewish town in the Ukraine or Poland, or the newly established collective farm of modern Palestine.

In matters of form, Palestinian literature has been deeply affected by many of the revolutionary tendencies in contemporary world literature. Throughout the 19th century it felt the impact of currents in European letters: German romanticism in the first decades, Russian realism in the lat-

ter half, and, to some degree, the *fin de siècle* toward the
turn of the century. Its Palestinian phase shows even more
markedly the effects of intimate contact with the various
trends in literary experimentation that in more recent years
have sought to mirror this changing world. French imag-
ism and symbolism, German expressionism and introspec-
tivism, post-revolutionary Russian iconoclasticism, all have
their representation in Palestinian poetry. The stream-of-
consciousness technique has penetrated into Palestinian
prose. In short, Hebrew literature in Palestine, far from being provincially self-contained, is an integral part of the
much wider life-stream of 20th century literary creativity.
Like it bewildered and warped in many respects, it is equally
audacious in its efforts to tell the story of modern man as he
struggles to extricate himself from the mazes of his half-
ruined past, and labors to decipher the glimmerings of his
new dawn. The Jewish element only heightens the human
confusion which it shares with all of modern literature, and
deepens the tone of its yearning for salvation. For that
reason alone, perhaps, it should be studied primarily for its
purely Jewish content, for its interpretations of the Jewish
past and present.

CHAPTER VI

New Directions
in Palestinian Literature

AN OCCASIONAL delving into the remote Jewish past in quest of subject matter for a poem, a novel or a play is not a new phenomenon in modern Hebrew literature. Modern Hebrew poetry actually began with the pseudo-epical or dramatic exploitation of biblical themes and characters as early as the 18th century, and not a few of its outstanding figures in the 19th occasionally resorted to the Bible for the same purpose.

What does impress the observer as new is that this attitude to the past has expanded in current Hebraic writing to include much more of Jewish history than biblical times alone. A somewhat inarticulate longing for a comprehension of the whole length and breadth of three thousand years of Jewish history seems to lie behind much of this present-day attraction to the past. All of Jewish history, as it were, strives in Palestinian literature to sanction the efforts which present-day Jewry is making to find salvation in its ancestral homeland. Jewish martyrology, it seems, tacitly blesses and wishes Godspeed to those superhuman efforts at self-redemption made by the Jew today. The biblical theme is still pre-eminent. It is in recent years, for example, that Hebrew poetry has been enriched by Jacob

Cohen's semi-allegorical dramatizations of the lives of David and of Solomon, and by the brilliant poetical plays of the late Mattathiah Shoham, which are modernistic studies of periods of biblical history as varied as those of Abraham and Moses, or Joshua and Elijah. But the attraction to later periods in Jewish history is just as marked.

There is the late Saul Tchernichovsky's poetical drama "Bar Kokhba," followed in rapid succession by his ballads on the martyrdom of Jewish saints in medieval Germany; and there are David Shimonovitz's veiled portrayals of the wanderings of the Kabbalists in the mountains of 16th century Safed, and the wistful soliloquies of "Israel Baal Shem Tov" by Jacob Fichman, in which the founder of Hasidism laments his fate, having "proved unworthy" to set foot upon the shore of the Holy Land. Indeed, this theme of historical Israel, of the wandering Jew praying for redemption, demanding and insisting upon it throughout the ages, is paramount in the literature created in the land of Israel or inspired by the achievements there in the past twenty-five years.

This penchant for the past is by no means so marked in Palestinian prose, although it, too, does not ignore the historical theme. On the contrary, a very impressive list of historical prose works produced in Hebrew in recent years could be drawn up at a moment's notice. Suffice it to mention A. A. Kabak's "The Narrow Path," a two-volume novel whose theme is the life of Jesus, and his trilogy celebrating the metamorphosis of the Marrano Jew Solomon Molcho into the martyred visionary who strives to "force the coming of the Messiah"; or Jacob Churgin's colorful novels and short stories based upon the life of Jewry in Central Europe in the late Middle Ages; or Asher Barash's tragically compact "Facing the Gates of Heaven," a study of the self-immolation of a Jew during the Cossack massacres of the 17th century, as he, the only survivor of a whole Jewish community, struggles to keep the sacred scrolls of the synagogue out of the reach of the rioting hordes; or S. Y. Agnon's beautiful *In the Heart of the Seas,* relating, in a semi-legendary manner, the miracle-studded journey to the Holy Land of the pious men of Buczacz (Galicia). Undoubtedly, Palestinian prose also tends to root itself in the pathos which pervades all of Jewish post-exilic history, to grasp as it were, the ultimate direction of its heroism. However, this strain, in the fiction at least, is largely drowned out by several more prominent voices which weave themselves into its polyphonic expression.

"Catholic Israel," to use Schechter's concept again, is definitely its main concern rather than Palestinian Jewry only. But it is the catholicity of Israel as it has crystallized into many different types, geographically rather than temporally or historically, that the novel and short story in the land of Israel chiefly seek to reproduce. Like earlier periods in modern Hebrew letters, Palestinian prose is still concerned with contemporary Jewry above all. The history of the modern Jew as he has evolved in the last one hundred and fifty years of the so-called period of emancipation still claims the best attention of the Hebrew novelist and short-story writer in the land of Israel.

The fortunes of the Jew as he seeks to integrate himself into the modern world about him, whether through self-abnegation or through self-discovery in the Jewish sense, the ruts and obstructions he encounters on either of these roads, still form the material of much contemporary Hebrew prose. In this respect, Hebrew fiction has attained a higher degree of catholicity in Palestine than it ever did before. Whereas some thirty years ago it was limited almost exclusively to the life of Russian-Polish Jewry, it has widened since to include practically every important center of the Diaspora. Germany, Austria, France, Switzerland, Turkey, even the United States (or rather the metropoles of these countries), each contributes today its local color to the short story and novel in Hebrew.

Illustrative of this trend is a prose work entitled "Under the Shadows of Kingdoms," by a prolific representative of the younger school of novelists, Hayyim Hazaz. Tracing the odyssey of a group of Jews, fugitives from pogromized towns in the Ukraine during the period of the Russian interregnum of 1917–1919, the author presents a kaleidoscope of the life of modern Jewry in a long list of European capitals as far apart and as diversified in civilization and atmosphere as Paris and Istanbul. On a much smaller scale, but tending to convey much the same impression, is a recent novel, "Seven That Started Out." In this narration, Yitzhak Shenberg, a highly endowed young writer, portrays vividly and yet serenely to the point of cruelty, the excruciating experiences of seven haunted victims of Hitlerism, six men and one young woman, hailing from different parts of Central Europe and differing in character and education as well as in Jewish outlook, as they strive in vain to steal across one frontier after another on their way to the land of Israel which beckons to them as their only haven of refuge. The widened dispersion of Jewry in the twenty-odd years between the two world wars has marked a corresponding widening of the territorial bounds of Hebrew prose.

Naturally enough, the specifically Jewish sympathies of Hebraic fiction have also broadened. Throughout the 19th century the Hebrew novel was militant in its criticism of the Jewish scene. Inspired by very definite tenets of a social faith, convinced that it preached the salvation of the group, it lashed out against what is considered social ills of the Jew's own making—against the obscurantism of Jewish orthodoxy, against the supineness of the Jewish masses under the "oppressions" to which they were subjected by the ghetto oligarchy, against the inertness of the community toward constant economic insecurity and cultural stagnation. But Hebrew fiction has lost much of this impatience with the reluctance of the Jewish people to face its fate with open eyes. It suffers with Jewry more than it condemns it. The pathos of Jewish disintegration in recent decades overwhelms it so completely that it scarcely can keep pace with the heart-rending process as it endeavors merely to record it.

Of course, the social-historical interpretation of the latest stages of the Jewish tragedy is Zionistic. In Hebrew fiction today every hue and shade of Jewish martyrdom, individual as well as collective, is traceable to Jewish homelessness as its prime cause. Not only the younger Palestinian prose writers, contemporaries of and frequently participants in the Halutz movement, but those of the older school, also, consciously and subconsciously share that philosophy of Jewish history. Isaac Dov Berkowitz has embodied it in his novel "Messianic Days," which presents the evolution into a Zionist of a highly intellectual and deeply Americanized Russian Jew who, late in his life matures, so to speak, even in the human sense, when he visits the land of Israel and comes to identify himself with the new life created there, for all his attempted scepticism and rigorous self-analysis. The same implications, more subtly conveyed, are discernible in a long novel by S. Y. Agnon, "A Guest for the Night," a fictionized study of the author's native town in Galicia which he, the greatest singer today of the piety of the Jewish ghetto, of its quixotic saintliness and quaint mysticism, revisits after the First World War to steep himself in the poignancy of its desolation.

Yet this "Zionistic" approach hardly ever asserts itself in concrete terms. Even Hayyim Hazaz, the severest as well as the most profound analyst of contemporary Jewish psychology, never preaches an explicit doctrine of Jewish self-improvement. By and large, Palestinian prose, for all its tacit gravitation toward Zionism, is the expression of the bewilderment of Jewish existence in the world rather than a conscious glorification of an idea set up as a guiding principle for confused Jewry. Characteristic of this tendency toward a more epic quality of writing is the last novel by A. A. Kabak, "The History of a Family." In the manner of a *Forsyte Saga,* he undertakes to trace the story of a Jewish family in the course of the last century or so, shifting from time to time the backgrounds of the several generations he depicts: from the small Jewish towns of long ago to the big cities of Eastern and Western Europe, with the ultimate intention of bringing their descendants to Palestine. His Jewish ghetto characters even in the period of early Russian Hasidism are drawn with the same understanding, indeed, with the same "lovingkindness" as are the modern characters in his Palestinian novel, "Between Sea and Desert."

One is particularly struck by the nostalgic tenderness with which the Hebraic narrative of late intuitively records its impressions of a Jewish life that is passing. It was Joseph Hayyim Brenner who once observed that while Yiddish fiction tended to romanticize the *staedtel*—the Jewish ghetto in Eastern Europe—its Hebrew counterpart was critically realistic in its treatment of it. Since then things have greatly changed. Many moods in current Hebrew fiction are engendered by the realization that the color, vitality and uniqueness of Jewish tradition, and even its breakup and the struggle between the new and the old in Jewish life, are rapidly lapsing into the oblivion of history and must be captured and preserved betimes.

No wonder the more individualistic masters of Hebrew prose in Palestine, Gershom Schofmann, Jacob Steinberg and Deborah Baron, for instance, also hark back to their pre-Palestinian past in the pursuit of manifestations of Jewish psychology more evanescent than those delineated by authors dealing with the solid folkways of historical Jewry or with the tangible conflicts which characterized its life in recent generations. No wonder so many writers of memoirs have emerged in Palestinian prose in the last two decades. Men of much smaller literary caliber than the late Shemarya Levin and Rabbi Jacob Mazeh respond to this blind urge to "memorialize" the glory that was the Jewish community in Poland, in White Russia or in the Ukraine. Vilna alone— "the Jerusalem of Lithuania"—which has been magnificently sung by Zalman Shneur in Hebrew, in a work named after it, has lately produced not only a goodly amount of verse by representatives of the youngest school in Palestinian poetry, but also several volumes of memoiristic writing. "The old order changeth"—and the pain of parting with it, it would seem, is nowhere more keenly expressed than in the forward-looking literature of modern Israel which, paradoxically enough, is at the same time the most daring challenge to the "old order" in contemporary Jewish history.

Quantitatively, then, if not strictly qualitatively, Palestinian prose is still far from being concerned exclusively with the local scene. Yet there are clear indications already abounding of the emergence of a narrative indigenous to the soil and air of modern Israel. Scores of short stories and sketches with the Palestinian daily scene as their subject matter and background regularly appear in the many periodicals of the country. A fair-sized library could be set up of collections of stories and some full-volume novels published within the last twenty-five years and dedicated to the new locale only.

In these prose works, the land of Israel receives more than a merely descriptive treatment. It is not just a question of "scenery"—of the incandescent gold and blue of the Palestinian day, the velvety darkness of its moonless nights, with their thickset, pear-shaped stars, of its strangely exhilarating yet exhausting *hamsins* in the spring and its torrential rains in the winter. The subtropical landscape, of course, contributes its share to the sense of the exotic which Palestinian prose has injected into modern Hebrew literature, rooted for over a hundred years in the more northerly scenes of the temperate zone. Yet, except in the novels and stories produced in the last ten years by young native Israelis, such as Moshe Shamir, Yigal Mosenson, Nathan Shaham, and above all the ingenious Yizhar (Smilansky), much of this is still purely decorative in the new Hebrew prose; the scenic element has struck deeper roots in Palestinian poetry. Nor is the local color of the more native prose of Palestine dominated by the oriental, frequently levantine, human element which it has discovered in the land. The eagerness with which not a few of the younger fiction writers attempt to study the Yemenite or the Bukharan or Persian Jew—not to say the Palestinian Arab—betrays rather a conscious impulse to exploit exoticism for its own sake than a creative self-identification with the characters they present. In this respect Palestinian prose has so far produced only one genuine artist of true magnitude. Judah Burla, a Sephardic Jew born in Palestine, is the only one among his contemporaries who has spontaneously exploited the wealth of color of his oriental milieu in numerous novels and stories. Fundamentally, Hebrew prose has "gone native" in Israel in a much deeper if less dazzling sense. It has introduced into Hebrew fiction a type of Jew unknown to it outside of Palestine—a Jew free from load, rid almost completely of the self-consciousness which is perhaps the most baneful connotation of Jewishness in the modern world.

In 1938 an anthology of Palestinian prose was published in Jerusalem, aiming, as its preface declares, "to present to the reader reviving Eretz Israel as mirrored in modern Palestinian literature." While only two of the twenty-six writers represented are native Palestinians, the striking feature of this compilation of complete stories and selections from longer works by so many prose writers of different backgrounds and of highly varying literary abilities is that they all register the revitalizing effect upon Jewish psychology of the sense of "homecoming"—of belonging. The student of Palestinian prose may question the assertion of the anthologists that "all the aspects of the new life created by the resurrected nation in its homeland . . . have already found their literary expression in Palestinian prose." Indeed, the opposite seems true, for—to quote

again—"this new Hebrew literature is still rooted in its ex-
ilic past." But another statement is equally true—"the
symptoms of the new life, the vibrations of the new atmosphere have already touched the heart of the modern Hebrew
author." Hebrew prose in Palestine has definitely come to
sense the meaning of "home" to the Jew who with his return loses "his over-spirituality as well as his fear," as Joseph Klausner expresses it in his introductory essay, "An
Ancient Nation Reviving." "The young Palestinian Jew,
truly neo-Jewish," he goes on to say, "does not regard the
world with eyes filled with fear, with eyes that find everything too complicated. The world is no longer strange, belonging to others. . . . It is a natural, simple, readily understandable world. It belongs to him—to the new Jew.
There are enemies, there are opponents, and he must defend himself against them because they want to rob him of
what is his, not because he, too, needs must live . . . in a
world that is not his." One may not agree with Klausner
that the Palestinian Jew, at least as he is reflected in Palestinian fiction, has really achieved the serenity of outlook attributed to him. He certainly does not seem to find the
world "simple" and readily understandable if one judges
him even by the portraits here presented. To the extent,
however, that the Jew discovers firm ground under his feet
in the land of Israel, he does evolve into the new Jew that
Palestinian prose seeks to portray.

Neither the variegated pattern of the "ethnic" composi-
tion of Palestinian Jewry, which is a veritable conglomera-
tion of "nations and tongues," though striving to become
"one people speaking one language," nor the immense
complexity of its group psychology as it seeks to become
"neo-Jewish," has as yet crystallized into sufficiently definite

forms to beget a mature prose literature. The pioneering effort itself, valiantly tackled by several able novelists: the naturalistic Eber Hadani, the more adventurous Avigdor Hameiri, and the somewhat mystically inclined Judah Yaari, and also David Maletz, keen observer of life in the Kvutzah, still awaits its epic delineation, the saga it deserves. Palestinian life is still too fluid to produce a seasoned narrative. Yet the native prose produced in the land of Israel has succeeded in capturing something of the ecstatic joy and pain inherent in the progress of an ancient people driven to rediscover its historic self in its ancient homeland.

In its social implications the poetry of Israel is definitely more Palestinian than the prose; its subject matter is almost exclusively the unique experience of a Jewry that is becoming Palestinian. Whether it sings times of relative peace or times of strife and struggle which are perennial, it seeks chiefly to express the essence of group life in the reviving country. Life in the land of Israel, according to its poets, is a peculiar amalgam of three ever-present emotions: an ineffable love for the land, a constant sense of danger threatening and a consciousness of incessant creative achievement. Of these, the love of the land of Israel is so elementary a concept in Jewish tradition that its new manifestations in Palestinian verse today may lose their distinctiveness just because they may be interpreted in terms of the traditional messianic yearnings in Jewish literature.

Yet the historic "love of the land" which the student finds in all of Jewish literature scarcely prepares him for the utter freshness which this feeling assumes in modern Palestinian poetry. For just as in our own day Israel has acquired a more concrete physical meaning to the Jew than ever before in his exile, so the poetic expression of that new meaning has become more immediate, more sensory and sensuous than it ever could have been in traditional Jewish literature. For eighteen hundred years, the mainspring of inspiration in Hebrew poetry whenever it sang of Palestine was the yearning from afar "to fondle the stones and caress the dust." It is the immediate contact with the land, the actual touch of its palpable self, that has found its many-voiced utterance in contemporary Palestinian verse.

The physical rediscovery of the Palestinian "glebe" has had an electrifying effect upon its poets. Inspired as they are by the realization that "the land" is actually being resurrected, that its soil sensitively responds to the hands of the Halutz who plants in it the seed of a new promise for Jewry, they still celebrate their intoxicating experience of being among the first in Jewish history to absorb the land with all their senses. Their art seems to have found its legitimate home, as they sing the "leprous" mountains of Judah reforested, the reclaimed marshes of the Emek, the drowsy palm tree in the blue and gold expanse of lonely stretches in the Negev, and the slab of live marble inserted into the wall of a building coming up in Jerusalem. No doubt Jacob Fichman, one of these new poets, was thinking of himself rather than of Ruth the Moabite, when in one of his dramatic poems he makes his heroine soliloquize as follows on first making acquaintance with the night of Bethlehem:

> Upon these fields of night, serenely pure,
> My feet tread lightly and securely, as if upon
> A soil most native, sacred from the day
> When first my star began to guide me hither.
> How friendly are the wings of night! My eye
> Distinguishes each bush, each rock, each clod,

As if a good and loyal hand were leading me.
Few are the days I have been here;
Yet like a grain of seed, untouched by frost,
This land so strange absorbed me lovingly. . . .
As if all that I knew and loved, from days
Of childhood rich in mystery till now,
Had ever sought but this one land of peace
Where my soul would be revealed to me
And where God's face would whitely glimmer forth.

And David Shimonovitz seems to identify himself with the hero of one of his idylls entitled "The Jubilee of Coachmen." Confessing that he found it at first painfully difficult to orient himself in "the land," at once so strange and so familiar, the "countryman," as the hero is called, a veteran of the pioneering movement in the first decade of this century, is made by Shimonovitz to recount his, and the poet's, own tribulations as a newcomer, when he says:

Long was my soul low-bent from the day I had come
    to the land.
Nature unrolled her book, but I could not read:
Strange the script was, and new; new were, and
    strange, its syllabications.
The mystery of the charactery held me spellbound;
    I felt its secret fascination,
But my heart had not learned how, without knowing,
    to leap in response to its call,
As does a bird into its nest. . . .
Thus I first understood that I still was in exile.
Gazing at the glorious palm, I yearned for the
    wistful white birch of the northland;
A blossoming winter contrived to entice me,

But I dreamed of the deserts of snow.
Long was my soul low-bent, and little, indeed, did
    I then comprehend
That nature ne'er hastes to cast off its veil in
    the sight of a stranger
Who will not, who cannot approach it more closely. . . .

A much more austere perception of the problem of adjustment to the new land than that suggested by either Fichman or Shimonovitz is to be found in the writings of the
younger school of Palestinian poets—Uri Zevi Greenberg,
Abraham Shlonsky, Yitzhak Lamdan, and Sh. Shalom, to
mention but a few of the better-known names of that group.

The latter hardly share the romanticism of Fichman's
conception of "the return" as the natural fulfillment of a
deep-rooted dream, a sort of "return of the native," in-
volving no struggle in the process of self-adaptation. But
they are just as far from the mood of Shimonovitz's equally
romantic portrayal of self-adjustment in terms of the newcomer's failure to penetrate directly into the "secrets" of
Palestinian Nature in an almost Wordsworthian sense.
These younger poets, children of the "wasteland" of the
years immediately following World War I, are too "wise"
to accept the relatively simple thesis that the problem of adjustment to the new life in the land of Israel is but one of
self-adaptation to the new landscape, of ceasing to dream of
the beauties of the snow-blown winter of Russia and of en-
joying the glories of its blossoming Palestinian counterpart. Their dream of the return was conceived in the apocalyptic darkly red glow of the "end of days" which came
upon massacred Jewry in Eastern Europe. The brittle, metallic cadences in which they sang their visions of the Redemp-

tion echoed the strokes of picks and shovels in the hands of
tattered and hungry Halutzim, fugitives from massacred
Jewish communities. Unromantic, almost as prosaically
sober as the barefoot Halutzim of whom they sang, were
these young poets of twenty years ago. They had little faith
in a dogmatized God, or in dogmatized nature, and still
less in dogmatizing man.

And yet the somewhat orgiastic quality of the poetry
they created has still something sacred about it. The deep
earnestness, the sense of dedication, will impress upon ages
to come the burning zeal and pain of postwar Halutziut—
its mystic faith, the idealism which enabled it to overcome
the hardships involved in the performance of its self-as-
sumed tasks. But the art of these young poets could not have
captured the spirit of Palestinian pioneering if it were not
endowed, as was the poetry of their older and more romantic colleagues, with a sense of complete self-identification
with the scene on which the historical drama of Halutziut is
enacted. It is once again the rediscovery in the flesh of the
ancient homeland that lends to Palestinian poetry a poignancy completely new in kind and quality, even when it
sings the age-old yearning for Zion. The realities of life on
the land have added an incisiveness to the theme of longing
for Zion unknown before in the best of Hebrew poetry.

Uri Zevi Greenberg, who among the ultramodernists has
presented in strident verse some of the most extreme ideas
of political Zionism, would have proved a hollow rhetori-
cian if the rich reality of the Halutz-scene had not given his
verse flesh and blood, a strangely shimmering vitality.
Here, for instance, is his manner of singing the Zionist
doctrine of "compulsion," of the hatred of the Jew, as
"forcing" Zionism upon world-Jewry:

Ah, well it is that we have forsaken Londons, Parises and New
   Yorks!

Ah, well it is that we have forsaken Europe and all the splendors,

And have become comrades to all the barefoot who burn in fever
   and whisper love to the sands and stones in Canaan.

   •   •   •   •   •   •   •

We were compelled to go forth and to leave behind all treasure,
   to set only bag upon the shoulder, to go forth with the kit of
   exile.

We sang songs also like recruits of an army, recruits of the army
   of the barefoot on the shores of the Mediterranean Sea.

They said: "Fever in Zion consumes its sick."

They said: "The Canaanite attacks upon the road and slays."

They said: "Jackals enter in under the blankets and devour the
   flesh of the living as he sleeps in his tent."

They said, they said, they said—but we went forth.

We were compelled to go forth. The earth cried out from under
   our feet, the beds trembled.

We ate, out of shame, the morsel to a satiety unto death.

We drank with a shudder, and we vomited like an adulteress.

And we saw in horror our own likeness in every outstretched
   figure upon a cross, until the cross and its agony rose up within the life of the spirit.*

Even when one reads Greenberg's lamentations in the same
poem over the fallen, desecrated state of Jerusalem, a theme
so frequent in traditional Hebrew poetry, one is struck by
the new vividness which it has assumed. That once again is
due to the poet's physical proximity not only to "Jerusalem
dismembered," but also to the whole scene which strives to
"raise up" the "City and Mother . . . from the midst of
the outpour of a rocky curse."

* From "Jerusalem," translated by Charles A. Cowen.

Undoubtedly, much of the personal element in Israeli poetry which celebrates the intensity of the pioneering effort itself, is due to the fact that not a few of the poets have themselves been Halutzim. All the lyricism of a Rachel could not have made her the sweet singer she was of the joy experienced by thousands of young neo-Jewish farmers as they attend to their daily chores, had she herself not imbibed the wistfulness and self-fulfillment she expresses in her "Dawn": *

> A jug of water in the hand, and on
> My shoulder—basket, spade and rake.
> To distant fields, to toil, my path I make.
>
> Upon my right the green hills fling
> Protecting arms; before me—the wide fields!
> And in my heart my twenty Aprils sing. . . .
>
> Be this my lot, until I be undone;
> Dust of the road, my land, and thy
> Grain waving golden in the sun.

Nor could the overtones of folk poetry have been achieved by much of the verse of some of the youngest writers in the country had they not themselves belonged to the "folk," to the masses of toiling young Jews and Jewesses, each of whom might describe the intimate experiences in words as simple and as moving as those of Abraham Braudes:

> For good I find it to broil in the sun of my land
> in the East,
> To press my lips to spouts of springs
> And bless my God and Creator.

* Translated by Maurice Samuel.

And good I find it to starve serenely with a
   dozen comrades,
Then feast upon a green tomato and burnt crust of
   bread,
And bless my God and Creator.

If in recent years Palestinian verse has tended to lose
some of the ruggedness and fervor which characterized it
in the twenties, this has largely been due to the fact that
most Palestinian poets have become city dwellers. It is only
in the poetry of men permanently settled in the Kvutzot,
such as Levy ben Amittai, S. Tenenbaum, and especially
Joshua Rabinov, that one still tastes the peculiarly earthy
exhilaration which Palestinian verse as a whole conveyed
in the twenties. Whatever the pros and cons of the tendencies toward individualism and intellectualism in the Palestinian poetry of the past decade, these tendencies are without doubt traceable to the increasing urbanization of the
poets of the country. Here we mention the modernists
Abraham Shlonsky (in his post-Halutz period), Jochebed
Bat-Miriam, Leah Goldberg, Ezra Sussman, Nathan Alterman, and Noah Stern, or the less daring experimentalists
Samuel Bass and Isaac Ogen.

Yet in its social aspect the poetry of the land of Israel
still is primarily the expression both of the conviction that
without Palestine Jewish historicity is doomed; and of the
realization that Palestine will become the home of hounded
Jewry. In the main, it still is the group utterance of a people
making its last-ditch stand for survival.

In the early twenties Yitzhak Lamdan made this idea the
theme of a long semilyrical, semidramatic poem, symboli-
cally entitled "Masada," which is the name of the last

fortress held by the Jews against the onslaughts of the triumphant Romans until, overcome by superior numbers, the defenders chose to die by their own hands rather than surrender. This poem has become the "classic" of the Halutz movement the world over. Many of the voices of "Masada" reverberate to this day in Israeli poetry, but its dominant chord is the one struck so somberly by Lamdan twenty years ago in some lines of the prayer with which he closes his poem:

Steady, O God, the footsteps of those who have slipped
    off the gallows
In strange lands, and have risen upon the walls of the
    fortress;
Steady them that they may not stumble and fall, for weary
    they are, and still stagger. . . .
Soften the hard rocks of Masada under their heads when they
    do fatigue:
Do not let the cold hail of despair blast that which they
    have sown here, the seed of souls and of dreams.
Bid, O God, many rains of solace to fall upon it, and may the
    dew fructify it at night,
Till it be rewarded with the promise of harvest! . . .
For if this time again you will not be merciful, O God,
Nor accept our dream, nor heed the offerings of those
    who strive to make the dream come true. . . .
O God, save Masada!

Viewed in its entirety, the literature which Palestine has produced territorially or inspired from afar within the last thirty years shows a highly checkered design of ideas and forms struggling for integration. Generally human and specifically Jewish needs, wants and conflicts, clashes between

individual and social drives; even the more or less super-
ficial inconsistencies between a deep-rooted nationalism
on the one hand and an equally potent consciousness of the
class struggle on the other, would in themselves tend to
make Palestinian imaginative writing complicated in its
experiential content. It becomes thematically even more
involved as it seeks to give expression to the new life germi-
nating in the revived homeland, while at the same time it
is impelled to interpret Jewish history, both past and present, in the Diaspora. The tangle of problems confronting
Palestinian authorship from the standpoint of subject matter has resulted in a no less bewildering maze of experi-
ments in new forms of literary expression. These, as has
been indicated, are for the most part strongly influenced by
experimentation in contemporary world literature, the impact of which upon Palestinian letters has been greatly en-
hanced by the hundreds of works translated into Hebrew in
recent years. Thus, in a relatively brief period, Hebrew
literature has achieved a degree of complexity which frequently amazes the reader acquainted only with the more
obvious aspects of its pre-Palestinian development.

Little wonder, then, that Palestine has not produced
much enlightened criticism, a type of interpretative study,
clearsighted enough to perceive the course which these letters have tended to follow. Even the trends stressed in these
pages have scarcely received the attention they deserve. Yet
they are fundamental for the understanding of the sense
of the new as well as of the complex which the literature of
Palestine conveys.

CHAPTER VII

Hebrew Literature
in the War Years

THE CATACLYSMIC upheaval known as World War II fell upon Israel with peculiar violence. Brief as was the period of the war years, they had an immense and many-sided repercussion on Hebrew literature. The impact of the catastrophe became, as one would expect, one of its major themes during the war.

"What of the future?" this literature seems to ask itself. "Watchman, what of the night?" What are the reserve energies Israel still can summon to survive the most terrible threat of destruction it has experienced in its long and tortured career? This implicit question it answers in three ways. There is Israel's historic will-to-be, almost elemental, almost biological—the Jew's eternal credo, "I shall not die, but live"; there is Israel's philosophic faith in the ultimate triumph of good; its eternal faith in the millennium which explains if it does not fully justify all suffering, universal as well as Jewish; and finally there is the position that Palestine holds in the present-day appraisal of Jewish history: it represents the promise of redemption, both Jewish and universal, much as it did with the second Isaiah, with Akiba, with Judah ha-Levi.

Such are the cardinal theses underlying the bulk of He-

brew literature during the war. Their very enumeration suggests the wealth and complexity of the material. But before
we proceed to examine them a word must be said biblio-
graphically about the literary output in Hebrew of the war
years. Astonishing as it may seem, at least some fifteen hundred volumes were published in Palestine during the war.
Nor can the fact be overlooked that in addition to these
different works in volume form, Palestinian Hebrew writers
have continued to supply uninterruptedly the needs of large
monthly and quarterly journals like *Moznayim* and *Gil-
yonot,* every issue of which compares favorably in intellectual and artistic merit with what the cultured reader in
America finds only in the university quarterlies and in the
intellectual reviews. One must also mention annuals like
Keneset and *Luah Haaretz,* and the *Davar* almanac, which
are veritable treasuries of thought, art and scholarship. And,
while the scholarly publications do not enter into the scope
of this volume, even a casual bibliographic review of
Hebrew letters during the war years cannot omit the mention at least of such scholarly journals as *Zion, Sinai, Lesho-
nenu,* and of scores of volumes of research and scholarly
editing done and published by such institutions as Mosad
Bialik and especially Mosad ha-Rav Kook.

There is still another consideration which adds to the
intricacy of the picture: the varieties of literary form have
their counterpart in a variety of literary schools. There is
the so-called Bialik school, with its humanism and its posi-
tivism of values, appreciation and expression; the iconoclastic school, the product of the nihilism and despair be-
queathed to literature everywhere by World War I and
roughly corresponding to the "lost generation" of the
twenties and early thirties in American literature; and,
youngest of all, the generation of Hebrew authors who have

come to reroot themselves in the social discipline of their grandfathers insofar as the affirmation of values is concerned, without actually having recovered the positivistic and humanistic values their fathers had scattered to the howling winds of the "wasteland."

Undoubtedly, a more thorough investigation of the subject would necessitate a systematic consideration of all the differences represented by the various schools, types and forms. However, in a survey such as this, similarity is perhaps more essential than difference, uniformity more revealing than diversity. In fact, the sense of deep somberness, not to say agony, which Hebrew war literature conveys in its entirety is only heightened by the fact that technical lines of demarcation between one school and another have tended to pale under the impact of the ineffable tragedy. The drama tends to become a lyric, the lyric a ballad, in this general urge to cry out the pain for which human expression in the noblest of forms is woefully inadequate. The classical serenity of a Jacob Cohen frequently becomes the strident, woebegone wailing of a Uri Zevi Greenberg. The wild imagery and involute moodiness of a rebel like Abraham Shlonsky assumes the simple character of tragic folk poetry, reminiscent of Sh. Shalom. The helpless watching of Israel being slaughtered has injected into Hebrew war poetry a strain of poignancy at once humble and desperate, which makes it seem to be surrendering almost consciously to the impersonal, undifferentiated grief of the human heart.

It would be a hopeless task to attempt to select samples of work characteristic enough of each of the poets who wrote them. Unsigned, they could hardly be traced to their particular authors even by scholars in present-day Hebrew writing. It is preferable to quote several selections from longer works and several complete lyrics in order to bring out more concretely the emotional temper of the poetry of the war years.

Jacob Cohen has been mentioned. He is, generally speaking, almost ascetic in his use of the Hebrew idiom. This aristocratic and classical tendency of avoiding ornate imagery and glamorously involved thought is still to be found in much of his war work, as in the following passage from "See the Evil." "And you," he addresses himself to Israel somewhat aloofly,

And you, the eldest of peoples, first to be
    pillaged ever and everywhere,
What hope still have you now in such a world
    and at such a time?
Upon whom, if not upon you, should the hand
    of evil descend with its overbearing force?
Over whom, if not over you, shall falsehood triumph? . . .

Perhaps it is the proud aristocracy of Israel, Israel "the eldest of peoples," which of necessity must be "first to be plundered ever and everywhere," rather than the poet's classicism that accounts for the restraint both of his protest and of his acceptance of Israel's bitter fate.

But compare this with the mood of another selection, this one from Cohen's "The Third Cry," to see how innate restraint gives way to a highly emotional treatment of the subject matter. Here, in a great imaginative work, Cohen uses the well-known late Midrash, "The Ten Martyrs," a versified version of which is recited on the Day of Atonement. The ten martyrs are ten renowned talmudic masters who have been condemned by the Romans to torture and death. They choose one of their number, Rabbi Ishmael "the High Priest," to ascend to heaven in order to learn whether their sentence was issued by God rather than by the Emperor

Hadrian. Arriving in heaven, he sees an altar close to the Throne of Glory, and is told by the archangel Gabriel that "the souls of the righteous are sacrificed on it daily" by the archangel Michael. Rabbi Ishmael understands, and descending to earth, tells his colleagues that the decree has already been written, issued and sealed. And they, realizing that theirs is to be a sacrificial death, resign themselves to their fate.

Rabban Simeon, the son of Gamaliel, was the first to die, and Rabbi Ishmael was so shaken by his martyrdom that he cried out to God "a loud and bitter cry": "A tongue that has interpreted the Torah in seventy tongues now wallows in the dust!" And heaven and earth quaked at his cry. Then Rabbi Ishmael himself went to the torture. And as the skin was slowly being drawn off his face by the skilled hand of the executioner, he remained silent until the hand reached that part of the head where rested the phylacteries —the symbol of man's communion with God through hallowed thought. And he who had resigned himself to physical death could not accept the desecration of Torah, and he cried out a second time, "a loud and bitter cry." The Throne of Glory shook and the angels around the throne remonstrated with God. "Is such a saint, to whom You have shown the treasures of the upper world and the mysteries of the lower, to suffer unnatural death at the hands of an evildoer? Is this the reward of sacred scholarship?" After some halfhearted attempts by God to vindicate the cruel act, a heavenly voice reverberated, saying, "If I hear another sound, I shall reduce the universe to primeval chaos." Then Rabbi Ishmael became silent. God himself, it would seem, is unable to square such desecration with the scheme of things. Yet God alone seems to know that there are periods in history when even the most sacred in man must

is redemption, complete and immediate redemption, that
he demands. And much in the character of the folk songs
attributed to him, Rabbi Levi Yitzhak stirringly exclaims
that if redemption be yet long-delayed—

> I shall cry out of all the abysses of the people's
>   sorrow that I carry in me;
> I shall cry that third cry which Rabbi Ishmael
>   the High Priest, never cried—
> Even if the heavens be torn into tattered shreds,
> Even if star upon star crumble, and become dust,
> And the universe revert to primordial chaos.

Classical serenity of mood, aristocratic self-restraint in
expression, are gone. The elementary folk motif, the un-
adorned hyperbole, which frequently takes the place of the
more subtle poetical metaphor in folk singing, have infil-
trated into the most Olympian moods of Hebrew expression. The poet, however individualistic, has become the
mouthpiece of the folk. Perhaps, even more strikingly, this
characteristic of Hebrew war poetry may be illustrated by
a quotation from a young modernist, Nathan Alterman,
generally given to a somewhat glaring picturesqueness in
his fantastic portrayals of landscape or mood and unre-
strained in his expression of personal or group experience.
Here is one of his war lyrics, sardonic and bitter, but so
simple in its construction and so direct in its folkloristic allusions, that even an English paraphrase conveys the pierc-
ing quality of "From All Peoples":

> When our children cried in the shadow of the gallows,
> We never heard the world's anger;
> For Thou didst choose us from all peoples,
> Thou didst love us and favor us.

For Thou didst choose us from all peoples,
Norwegians, Czechs and Britons;
And when our children are marched to the gallows,
Jewish children, wise Jewish children,
They know that their blood is not counted in the
    bloodshed—
They only call back to their mothers: "Mother,
    don't look!"

How great the concern for paintings and sculptures,
Treasures of art, lest they be bombed;
While the art treasures of baby-skulls
Are dashed against walls and pavements.
Their eyes only speak: "Don't look, mother,
Veterans we are, soldiers renowned—
Only undersized!"

Their eyes speak yet other things;
God of the patriarchs! We know
That Thou didst choose us from all children,
That Thou didst love us, and favor us.
That Thou didst choose us from all children
To be slaughtered before the Throne of Glory;
And Thou dost gather our blood in buckets
For there is none else to gather it.

And Thou dost scent it like the perfume of flowers,
And dost sponge it up in a kerchief;
And Thou wilt seek it from the hands of them that
    murdered
And from the hands of those that kept silent.

Jews in the land of Israel experienced the extermination
of European Jewry from day to day and from hour to hour
as if undergoing the continued torture in their own flesh.

No wonder one hears a delicately laconic poet like Mordecai
Temkin almost whisper, in his "God's Wrath Has Overcome Us," the helplessness of Israel, from within the elec-
trified barbed-wire fences of the concentration camp:

> In His lap we place our heads with the flock
>   of tremulous stars—
> Mute, frightened like them,
> And as lonely, as forsaken!

No wonder that this poet, whose work contains some of the
deepest religious feeling in contemporary Hebrew verse,
apologizes to God on behalf of surviving Jewry, more specifically, the Palestinian community, in a poem entitled
"Prayer," from which the following is quoted:

> Forgive us, merciful God, that we are safe,
> That our cities have been spared,
> That they teem with humanity, with children,
> And none to make them afraid.

How characteristic is this mood of the Jews in Israel,
searching their heart in the glow of the conflagration which
consumed European Jewry while Palestinian Jewry itself
survived in safety, in the shameful safety of its helplessness.
We cannot here go into the carefully recorded and authenti-
cated facts which testify to the heroic efforts made by Palestinian Jewry to save as many Jewish lives as possible from
the clutches of the Hitlerian ogre—the maintenance of constant communication lines with the underground in Europe; of connections with doomed Jews in the concentration
camps of Europe; the organization of self-defense and revolt in the ghettos. This phase of active Palestinian participation in the tragic efforts made by European Jewry not to

die ignominiously is a chapter which the historian will regard as one of the most glorious in the chronicles of Jewish
martyrdom. The desire of the poet, of the man of letters
generally, to preserve in the mold of the written word the
torturing dread of Jewish extinction is no more than the
heartfelt need of the survivor to identify himself with the
suffering of his slaughtered brothers.

And not only pure literature expresses this need. There
are also numerous books and essays which are wholly documentary in character: chronicles, diaries, testimonials, and
eye-witness accounts, many of them translated into Hebrew
from the original Russian, Yiddish, Polish and German,
and all of them records of Hitlerism on the rampage. This
mass of documentary material has been published by practically every thriving publishing house in Palestine and it was
obviously marketable. It, too, like the copious records of the
Jewish tragedy in fiction and poetry, is an expression of the
Palestinian Jew's desire for self-identification with the experience of European Jewry. That such self-identification is
humanly impossible, since neither thought nor word is capable of bringing it about, Hebrew writers know very well.
Here are the words of one poet, Benjamin Tannenbaum:

How dare I dip my pen in blood, how dare I kindle my
    word with the fire of the cursed conflagration?
There is no fitting stir of feeling; no word, nor phrase
To utter the affliction of man, the affliction of a
    people wallowing and suffocating in their own blood,
The disaster of a reduced, low-bent generation, whose sun
    has darkened in broad daylight,
Who by the light of its burning world quickly moves toward
    the abyss.

Furthermore, none is so deeply ashamed as the Hebrew war

poet himself of this urge to recount the horrors; and he often confesses this sense of shame, as does Tannenbaum in the last stanza of the poem:

> How dare I dip my pen in blood while it is holy blood
>   that is shed?
> I am ashamed to dip the pen in it, to polish with it
>   nicely symmetrical utterance:
> Blood-dripping has no rhyme; there is no metaphor
> That may atone for a tear shed, a stifled groan or
>   wailing;
> Blood has a language all its own—each tone replete
>   with orphanhood and bereavement.
> It howls to me from the ground, and its howling will
>   not be silenced.

Occasionally, as in the following rare lyric by Leah Goldberg, one notes the wistful, childlike wonder whether the horrors may not be forgotten some day, in a world restored to its pristine glories, the elementary glories of life in its simplest joys, its purest and deepest satisfactions.

> Will days, indeed, yet come in forgiveness and grace,
> When you will walk in the field, will walk like a
>   simple-hearted wayfarer,
> With clover leaves stroking your bare feet,
> With the stubble sweetly stinging?
>
> Or rain overtake you with its throng of drops
> Beating upon your shoulders, chest, neck and fragrant
>   head;
> And you will walk in the wet field, quietude expanding
>   in you
> Like light in the skirts of a cloud?

And you will breathe in the smell of the furrow,
   breathe and be calmed,
And you will see the sun in the golden mirror of the
   puddle—
All things simple, and alive, and you may touch them,
And you may, you may love?

You will walk in the fields alone, unscorched by the
   heat of the blazing fires,
On roads that bristled with horror and blood;
And in purity once again be meek, and submissive,
As is a blade of grass, as is mere man?

It is not only the hope, faintly breathed by this dreamlike mood, that man once again may become "mere man," waking from the nightmare to the eternal joys of being, that makes this poem so moving. Its pathos stems chiefly from the sense of tacit yet terrifying doubt lest man never again become "mere man" that may touch "all things simple," and "may . . . may love." The doubt is the more terrifying to the Hebrew poet, since the restoration of "mere man" to the order of "all things simple" hardly carries the promise of the same restoration to the Jew, who may be excluded even from a restored world. He may even then remain in his utter loneliness, with the eternal reverberations of Jeremiah's laments in his soul. This probable continuation of the Jewish historic fate is poignantly brought out in the poem "To Those Who Return from Battle," by another woman poet, Jochebed Bat-Miriam:

To them, brass bells,
Sounds of festive chiming,
From coast to coast on every continent,
Will sing triumph from afar.

Cities well-born and famous,
Will wave flags of welcome
As if renouncing triumphant force,
And about to be inscribed in a new page.

Nameless, unbeknown,
They will march past,
Their eyelids golden with dust,
As if returning to a fairy tale, unfamiliar,
As if sailing away from the vision of an island deleted.

Aside, away from drum and music,
Will merge in city and garden
A cornstalk—in embroidered apron,
A woman trailing a cloud. . . .

But there from beyond some constellation
In the white-heated path of the sky,
Looking upon all the smoking remains of the
    conflagration,
Exhaling all the desolation and ruin,

Vacuous, bronzed,
The tablet of Jeremiah looms silent—
Wildly flown in the dark, its letters
Pursue, still pursue my people.

It is this gruesome realization of a people ever alone, ever pursued by Jeremiah's abysmal threnodies even while the world welcomes its returning heroes—the champions of a better, a nobler world—that forbids forgetfulness to the Hebrew poet; as in this stanza by Samuel Bass:

All that was but yesterday: human yearning, prayer and
    trust,
A bit of ecstasy, of song and pain—the daily bread

Of millions of my brothers, has suddenly become a
    dunghill;
But another while—and all this will seem so far away.

And once again, perhaps, hands will be washed clean by
    this sinful generation,
And unhesitatingly will it sit down to its morrow's repast;
And again a father will fondle his child with heroic song,
And tell him nothing about a trampled child.

Only we here alone will turn our glance back;
In the sweeping surge of the morrow, in the tumult
    of the day,
We shall suddenly freeze for a moment and remember—
The butchery of Jews, the native home forever bereaved.

No blossoming shall drown the image;
No luxurious visions man may conjure tomorrow;
Cursed be the grandchild that will seek to induce
    forgetfulness,
That will forget this generation, the tears and the blood.

A good deal has yet to be said in a later chapter about the
opposite strain in Hebrew war literature; for not only the
note of despair is sounded. There is also the note of hope.
To suggest its quality, and to end this analysis of the impact
of the war on Hebrew writing in a major key, we quote the
following verses by Jacob Fichman, written May 1, 1942,
and entitled "Remember, My Heart."

Remember, my heart, that besides the beasts of prey,
Who vision the fall of man,
There still are millions of hearts that love,
That struggle in the surging billows of blood;
    Remember those who have joined battle for man.

Remember, my heart, all those who stand
In the flames facing the foul foe—
All who have rushed forth to save those that may perish,
All whose heart has not remained silent in the dark;
    Remember those who have joined battle for man.

Remember those who trudge in the scorching sands,
Who leave their traces in deep, heavy waters;
For the noble hearts that still are there
Remembering them—let us pray for them.
    They are the ones who have joined battle for man.

CHAPTER VIII

Premonitions of Disaster

THE LARGE output, the variety of theme, form and mood, and the generally high quality of Hebrew war literature and especially of Hebrew war poetry noted in the preceding chapter, was noted also by Palestinian critics. But strangely enough the Palestinian public, which one would expect to find stirred by this powerful expression of the helpless anguish, the lonely forsakenness and the mass destruction of European Jewry, was not satisfied with the response of its writers to the crisis. Palestinian readers, it seemed, were disappointed or resentful over the supposed nonexistence of the multitudinous mournful, violent, philosophic or interpretative productions they must have been reading from day to day. What was wrong, they asked repeatedly in the daily press, with those whose function it was to record, interpret and preserve the drama of Israel's vicissitudes, and who in this instance were not rising to the task. The complaints and the replies developed into a considerable controversy joined in by the professional critics.

In an article in the Davar Almanac *Tav-Shin-Dalet* for 1944, Immanuel Ben-Gurion summed up the attitudes that produced this unwarranted criticism and replied to it. There were people, he said in effect, who demanded that the creative writer enlist as it were militarily and obey the command of the hour; and who attempted to rationalize this demand by pointing to the unique situation of Jewry, a people predominantly in exile—victims of war but denied all creative war ecstasy and an equal participation in the war with its allies. While the enemy is apparent, the true friend must remain invisible. Yet what should this war be for the Palestinian Jew but a holy war consciously undertaken, which should give rise to its own inspired bards.

It was true, he conceded, circumstances were not favorable for the emergence of an adequate war literature in Hebrew. The tensions of the situation were so great as to constitute an assault on the unity of the will, on the health of the creative instinct. But, astonishingly, in spite of all this, there was "war literature, poetry and prose, documentary and artistic record, matter and spirit. It has been created unawares," he wrote, "it has grown in the natural course of self-expression; drop by drop, its tide has risen and surged forth. Paradoxically enough, our weakness has become our strength. . . . This literature draws its message from the very roots of our unique position, from our utter helplessness and discouragement."

In retrospect it seems that the fact that Palestinian war literature in its rich abundance did not satisfy, even quantitatively, the Palestinian reader's hunger for self-identification with all the horror of recent Jewish experience was due primarily to a peculiar situation in past literary history. Hebrew literature during the war continued to present Jewish fate and destiny in terms and modes in which it had envisaged Jewish fate and destiny for a long time before the tornado sweepingly overwhelmed world-Jewry. The fact is that for several decades before the advent of Hitlerism at its worst, for several decades before World War II, Hebrew letters had frequently voiced premonitions of the storm about to break. As a result, the Palestinian reader, with his sensibilities long attuned to the warnings of danger in his literature, scarcely found anything new or even surprisingly stirring in the emotional and imaginative recordings of the earthquake for which he was so well prepared. The Hebrew reader's sensibilities, like the literature itself, had in a way foretasted the catastrophe long before its arrival; and, terrible as the reaction to the precipitation of the tragedy has been, ample as has been the effort to record the tragedy, the written word during the war years only echoed voices that long before the war sounded the same despair.

One need read only Tchernichovsky's "Martyrs of Dortmund" (*Haruge Tirmunia*), written in 1937, to perceive what is meant by premonitions of the catastrophe discernible in the Hebrew poetry of the thirties. The details of this ballad are perhaps too horrible to quote. The poet himself describes them in his introductory lines as things "a human being cannot hear, cannot make others hear, unless he has gone out of his mind." Yet this poet of beauty and strength, the singer of the eternal joy of living, a true Renaissance figure in the world literature of the last half century, lavishes the best of his imagination upon the gruesome details of the torture and slaughter of the medieval Jew, Elijah Hasid, and of his wife and children; details which, in the poet's own words, "only a brain stricken with insanity can picture," details which Hitlerian Germany so realistically enacted upon modern Jewry. This ballad, written in 1937 and dedicated to the memory of a medieval saint, is the forecast not only of the butchery that took place a few years later, but of the technique of the butchery in the best style of Maidanek. The monologue delivered by this medieval martyr after he has been dug up from the grave where he has

lain all night bleeding and almost dead, with his dead wife
and children, is characteristic of the premonitions of the
disaster in prewar Hebrew writing. And no contemporary
of the disaster has produced a more shattering cry of misery
than the blasphemous words of Elijah Hasid when he is
shoveled out of the earth by his tormentors and commanded
by them to worship "their God," who has obviously tri-
umphed over his.

> He looked at the speaker and smiled:
> "Right you are! God triumphed over god.
> There is no God, there isn't. That's it.
> There is no God. Neither Jewish nor Christian.
> Cannot God answer?
> Cannot God have mercy?
> Cannot God work a miracle?
> And when my lungs, hungry for
> A whiff of air, burst with pain,
> And when I gnawed at my fingers with my teeth,
> So that pain might still pain,
> So as to quench my thirst with my blood,
> Where was He? Where—the Omnipotent?
>
> .   .   .   .   .
>
> There is no God! There is Satan alone!
> He guides the world in his insanity,
> He rules over all the sons of Satan,
> The monsters. You offer me life—
> Life for what?
> Only that I, too, become
> Among you, like you, a beast breaking loose. . . .
> Oh, slaughter me right now, immediately—
> Else I, too, shall become a wolf,

> A mad dog among leprous dogs,
> Human filth, all foul.
> There is no God. Perhaps
> There is no Satan, either, and there is . . . there is
> In the world—woe is me!—falsehood alone,
> It, great falsehood only.
> Man that is vanity, and no more, forever."

Paradoxically, the last two words of the poem are *Yitgadal ve-Yitkadash* (May the name of the Lord be exalted and sanctified). Tchernichovsky, the great yea-saying poet of contemporary world literature, however pagan, however sensuous, could not but reaffirm his faith in life, even though his hair must have stood on end when he wrote that ballad. Yet the reaffirmation of his faith is not personal, is not subjective; it is collective; it is the traditional Jewish affirmation of Eternal Being on the very brink of perdition.

It is difficult not to be overawed by the group intuition which Hebrew literature in the thirties so often manifests. To the nearsighted, the disturbances in Palestine are but a local affair, a repetition of a set pattern of events affecting Palestinian Jewry only and scarcely to be related to the larger pattern of the apocalyptic evil whose heavy shadow already darkened the earth. But Hebrew writing registers only too keenly an awareness of the true meaning of those local events. Its Jewish instincts speak forth on behalf of threatened world-Jewry when it seeks to read in them signs of the not-too-far-off calamity. Tchernichovsky, who in those years writes ballad after ballad commemorating Jewish martyrs in medieval Germany, produces also numerous lyrics in which the "local disturbances" are interpreted as a prediction of the re-enactment of those medieval horrors upon Jewry the world over. The vulture which in one of

the lyrics he observes circling over the mountains of Judah
in January, 1936, however literally a "vulture"—a large
bird of prey whose symmetrical floating in the air merely
inspires his keen admiration—subtly transmutes itself into
an almost ghoulish portent. The first stanza of this short
poem should be compared with the second and the third:

> A vulture! A vulture over your mountains! A vulture
>   flying over your mountains!
> Languorous and lithe—for a moment it seems but to
>   float;
> It swims, it floats, in a sea of blue, alert to gleeful
>   music at the crossroads in the sky;
> The sky itself but music enchanted, mute festiveness.
>
> A vulture! A vulture over your mountains! A vulture
>   flying over your mountains!
> Straight of limb and heavy-pinioned, black of feather
>   and broad of wing;
> Tense, it sweeps; an arrow aimed, a vulture riding
>   in circuitous curves;
> Tracking its prey from above in the meadow below, in
>   the crevice of the rock.
>
> A vulture! A vulture over your mountains, a vulture
>   flying over your mountains!
> Languorous and lithe—for a moment it seems but to
>   float.
> O, Earth! A vulture over your mountains—a heavy
>   shadow cast upon your face,
> Cast by wings of a monster gigantic, stroking the
>   mountains eternal.

Unconsciously almost, fascinated, as in a terrifying dream,
the poet sees the vulture in all its languor and litheness

transformed into a "monster gigantic"; and just as unconsciously, addressing Palestine by the anonymous *Eretz* (earth), he reads into the heavy shadow cast by the bird's wings a significance which extends beyond the territorial bounds.

Much less allegorically but with the same effect of nightmarish fascination, Gershom Schofmann, a highly subjective impressionist, treats in his sensitive prose the same theme of the larger Jewish implications of Jewish Palestine in the state of siege brought upon it by the Arab disturbances which broke out in 1936. Apparently a guest at the time at one of the newly-founded besieged Kvutzot, he writes a sketch entitled, "Not to Sleep, Not to Sleep!" which is here cited in full:

" 'Not to sleep, not to sleep!' the little boy cries and seems to beg for his life as he is being carried in his mother's arms from his parents' shack, where he has been visiting toward evening, back to the children's home. He is eager to remain here with daddy and mother, to stay awake, awake.

"Shadowlike, members of the Kibbutz wander about in the falling dusk, among the shacks, among the large packing cases brought over by German refugees, among canvas tents. Singly and in couples, they tramp aimlessly in the deep sand. 'I knew her in Warsaw . . .,' one of them relates. The large aluminum tea kettles sparkle in the lit-up kitchen. For a moment, the door of the shower-house opens and a stripped young fellow is seen inside, shuddering a little.

"The guards are at their posts, and the large revolving searchlight guides its belt of brightness across the fields beyond, illuminating a kind of peculiarly reddish aftergrowth which is saturated, as it were, with the blood of battles of long ago. Farther, farther, way beyond, to the ends of the world, throw your searching brightness! For the whole world—is one camp of the enemy. On all sides, all around, they lie in ambush for us. They cannot endure it that we have found something of a foothold; they cannot endure it that we still breathe a little. It is not booty and spoils that they seek; nor to inherit our possessions. It is just that our life itself, our mere being alive hurts them.

"We must draw closer together, our boys and girls, ever closer together. We must stand guard, be on the lookout, all eyes, to pierce the treacherous darkness. We must intensify our alertness a hundredfold—not to sleep, not to sleep! ! One's heart so trembles for the children, for the girl one loves, and there is a desire stirring to protect them with one's own body, right now. . . . For the savage will not spare the most tender, the most gentle among us. He will not spare any!

"Out of the thick darkness the sandbags glimmer at the bottom of the fence—those eternal sandbags, heavily piled one on top of the other, that do not permit us to forget the situation. Remote and cold and indifferent, the stars are radiant in their courses—those stars of Deborah's. Remote, and cold, and indifferent, and no longer reliable, as they were in the days of Sisera, when the battle now blazes. . . . Singly, and in couples, the members of the Kibbutz tramp in the deep sand. 'I knew her in Warsaw . . .,' one relates. A girl's head bending over a book is seen by the light of the lamp through a shack transom. Stripped, all bare, a lonely young fellow shudders under the shower. The revolving searchlight illumines the reddish plain smeared with the blood of battles of long ago; it strains to extend its belt of light farther, over the whole hostile area, all around, farther, farther, to the ends of the world; and the little boy, being carried to the children's home, screams, begs for his life: 'Not to sleep, not to sleep!' "

Thus it is no exaggeration to say that long before the war Hebrew writers were almost clairvoyant in their forebodings of the tragedy that was to befall Jewry the world over. As far back as 1904, Bialik, in his well-known lyric "O Heaven, You Must Pray for Me," prophetically exclaimed on behalf of all Jewry, "To me the whole world is one gallows." And he also challenged the platonic idea of justice to prove its case by materializing for the Jew immediately, blasphemously exclaiming in his anguish:

> If not until after I have been deleted from under
> the heavens justice appear,
> May its throne be destroyed forever.

But in the course of the thirty years that followed, particularly during the twenty years between the two world wars, Hebrew literature, in prose even more than in poetry, repeatedly and voluminously gave utterance to the conviction that Israel was being condemned to death by a world gone mad or, as the liberal-minded historian would put it, by a world contorted with the pangs of a new birth. Meir Seco's and Abraham Freiman's stories of the extermination of Ukrainian Jewry in the interregnum between the overthrow of czardom and the establishment of the Soviet regime; Avigdor Hameiri's tales based upon his experiences as an officer in the Austro-Hungarian army, of sadism practiced upon the emancipated and semi-emancipated Jews of Central Europe; the studies of Hayyim Hazaz on the fate of a Jewry "in the shadow of seven kingdoms," the homeless, humiliated Jewry all over Europe, from Paris to Berlin and from Berlin to Constantinople; Agnon's later work, especially his masterful long novel already mentioned, "A Guest for the Night," in which the author reincarnates in his own flesh and psyche the slow dying of all that was great and noble in Jewish existence in Eastern Europe, as he revisits, in the twenties, his home town, the hallowed haunts of his childhood dreams and visions—in all of these, whatever the plot of the story, the personal approach of the author, the literary gifts, the psychological and political affiliations, his diagnosis of the Jewish scene always leads him to the edge of the abyss into which European Jewry is being flung.

These forebodings of the catastrophe, while chiefly concerned with its consequences to Jewry, seldom fail to encompass the implications for all humanity. Jewish apologetics have always found it absurdly necessary to explain, to frightened, self-negating Jews above all, that so-called Jewish particularism never was the negation of universalism; that the prophets and psalmists, the rabbis and medieval pietists, singers and philosophers, were not only Jewish patriots but also humanists and lovers of mankind. Modern Hebrew literature, more deeply rooted in Jewish tradition than even the Jewish scholar frequently seems to know, is also humanistic in outlook, even while painfully aware of the shame of its unrequited love—its unwarranted faith in man. One should reread Zalman Shneur's "The Middle Ages Are Approaching," a poem which he wrote in 1913, before World War I.

> The Middle Ages are approaching—do you heed, do
>   you sense, O man of soul,
> The stir of their creeping dust, their distant
>   smell of sulphur?

> And that intangible oppression in the air, in the
>   heart, everywhere,
> As if at an oncoming eclipse—when houses turn
>   ashen-gray and shaky,
> The blue sky—leaden; the cows low restlessly with fear,
> And grass and tree assume a silvery hue, the tinge of
>   cellar-damp,
> And human faces freeze, and look strange as do wax
>   masks? . . .

For a brief spell, Shneur feels, man had come to believe that
the medieval monster was dead, that the Renaissance had
killed him, mounted him in the museum of liberalism with
a stuffing of culture, science, democracy and the self-deter-
mination of nations. But, the poet declares,

> He, the monster, is about to crack the casting, overgrown
>   with gardens and cities;
> He is about to break his civilized fetters. . . .
> And the scrolls of human love and the swaying flags
>   of liberty,
> Will be scattered in all directions, like children's
>   toys in the storm.
>
> Set themselves up as heirs of Caesar and Caesar's
>   sword,
> With armies fighting for their glory, equipped with
>   weapons of destruction
> Cast in brass, and preparing a butchery of nations,
> At the least wave of their hand. . . .

Again, Israel is to be the first victim of this resurrected
monster of medievalism: a medievalism which has but
changed its name, no longer calling itself religion but "pa-
triotism." Yet, note in the name of what ideal Shneur urges

Israel to equip itself to face the monster of resurrected medievalism:

Your task is not yet fulfilled, O eternal people!
The play has not yet reached its end.
The heavy curtain has not yet been lowered; millions
  of eyes are still uplifted
To you, and to the climax of the drama, eyes of friend
  and foe alike.
If nations, invidious, whistle in scoffing, do not
  lose heart;
Remember, their uncircumcised hearts, too, secretly
  look forward
To the end of the sublime performance which, for
  thousands of years, has unfolded before them.
You must still go forth. You shall yet go forth,
  appear on the world scene,
And your warm strong voice pierce the shriekings of
  nations
Till they grow mute, dazed and pale at the sight of
  your welling courage,
At the sight of your inspirited essence, as you bring
  to a close the drama of history;
Till they hide their abashed faces in trembling hands,
And kneel, and weep self-forgetfully, the weeping of
  eras confessing their sins;
Then you will order the curtain to come down, as your
  agitated spirit quiets;
And remain alone with your victory, ere the whole world
Passes on to the period of great brotherhood, to a
  God unforeseen by prophets,
And to a life undreamed of by singers. . . . Prepare for
  the lofty scene . . . O Israel!
The days of transition are approaching. . . .

Thus, even in Shneur, generally Nietzschean in his not infrequent disgust with man, the theme of the Dark Ages approaching strangely evolves into the "days of transition . . . approaching," with Israel announcing the new "great brotherhood" of man and "a God unforeseen by prophets." Even here the immolation of Israel is tacitly accepted if not quite justified by the arrival, for all mankind, of "a life undreamed of by singers." In fact, if, as Shneur puts it in the last section of his poem, human salvation is unachievable; if, with the advent of an era of new medievalism,

> Doom is decreed upon all and everything,
> So that the light, once dimmed, never again
>   shine forth,
> And you be swept along by the inexorable wheel
> To be ground by its teeth forever, to oil its
>   axle with your blood. . . .

—even then Israel is to die only when bringing down with it a world that will not be retrieved, that will not be redeemed. Jews must die then,

> As the last clean humans round the abominable wheel.
> Enough dying like martyrs, leaving the world to the
>   unclean!
> You shall die the death of all creators, who consume
>   and are consumed in the world
> For the sake of the new arising, with innocence, with
>   pristine mystery in their eyes. . . .

CHAPTER IX

The Meaning of the Disaster

THE WORLD must not be left to uncleanness. Hence the pertinacity with which the modern Hebrew poet urges on the Jew to continue against all odds, certain that the Jew will continue. Whether one likes it or not, the so-called "mission idea" somewhat vacuously and self-consciously preached by Reform Judaism secretly feeds much of the best-inspired and most hopeful poetry in Hebrew, as it attempts to appraise Jewish misery and find some explanation for it. Of course, the doctrine is not explicit; and, needless to say, it differs profoundly from the abstractly held tenet of "Israel's mission," in that Israel is accepted—proudly accepted, believed in, and prayed for—as a distinct and distinctive entity, regardless of its tacitly assumed function in human history. Nevertheless, one is often struck by this curious source of comfort which the Hebrew poet ever rediscovers with unending faith: Israel is bruised and bleeding because the world must learn to stop bruising, to end bloodshed and pain. Whether one likes it or not, and Hebrew criticism, it seems, has preferred not to note the phenomenon, the tacit assumption in Hebrew poetry is still the old Judah ha-Levi idea that Israel is to mankind what the heart is to the human organism. It inevitably must register the pain, the disease affecting any part of the organism that is mankind. It is

strange to hear Zalman Shneur, the confirmed poet of the
ego, urging Jewry in the poem cited: "Neither to stand in
the devious way [of the wheel, which he makes represent
the destructive onrush of medieval barbarity] nor to spin
along with it." For,

> You must be the conscience of the world, the forgotten
>   sense of shame to the nations.
> You must sew fig leaves together to cover their
>   nakedness. . . .
> Ye are the salt of the earth. . . .
> Let it make more palatable your unsavory existence.
> You are the radiance of the world—emerge then from the
>   dungeons of the nations!
> You have set up God in their skies—let him shine forth,
>   if shine he still may.
> Do not sell your first birthright to Esau for a porridge
>   of lentils—
> Do not sell your gentle birth for a tottering shack
>   at the crater of a raging volcano.
> Do not leave it to nations that do not know you to
>   solve the ancient riddle of your being. . . .

Indeed, to the extent that Hebrew literature in our day
has made the effort to understand the why and wherefore
of Jewish suffering, it has tended to revert to this time-
honored explanation: that Israel is a riddle to the world
that must be done away with since it is so disturbing, yet—
at the same time—a riddle which carries within it the solution of the very ills that afflict the world. Generally speaking, even the fiction, always more sober than poetry, more
likely to keep away from the metaphysical, has not shunned
this theme and has even tended to satirize it. In poetry es-

pecially, however, this idea—harking back to the prophets —that Israel's election means both the slowly waking conscience of the world and the victimization of Israel by that forever immature collective conscience, has produced some remarkable work in the very period we are discussing.

Fundamentally, this theme is the mainspring of the inspiration of Mattathiah Shoham, whom only the cognoscenti—Bialik among them—have as yet acknowledged as one of the finest poets of our time. Shoham, most of whose work is in the form of dramatic poetry, has written magnificently on biblical themes. These dramas, so rich in color, so subtle in characterization that they can stand upon their own validity as works of art, still convey to the reader a strong impression of the poet's consciousness of the position held by Israel in human civilization. Israel's historic voice as heard and interpreted by Shoham is always the admonition that neither will to power and achievement alone, nor the artistic and philosophic urge alone, leads to the happiness which humanity so blindly pursues. As Shoham sees him, historic man has endeavored throughout the ages to indulge those urges as ends in themselves—only to drown out his own dim consciousness that he expects something more of himself for the attainment of a balance. Historic man resists the nascent perception that this balance can be attained only by means of widening sympathies with that which is not quite the self, which is the *alter* ego; not really one's own self, yet so very much like it, so very much part of it. Israel alone has long known this, beginning with Abraham who, in Shoham's "Iron Gods Thou Shalt Not Make unto Thee," declares: "I know, you have chosen me, my God, to pour into me the first-ripened wine of mature blood, that I may be first to all those who are come of age to

bear man's pain and vision, and to join ranks in the struggle for man's ultimate end—to walk alone as God's firstborn, without mediating angel. For, first to me among men,
have you been not mere ruler of all, nor mere fretful Deity:
You were revealed in my spirit; and it—my spirit—of a
sudden tingled with song at the wonder of its own emergence and at its ultimate meaning. And ever since, my spirit
does not know who it is but you in it, and who—but you—
am I. . . ."

This is a thesis that does not require too much expatia-
tion: Man's soul, the ego, is God—God revealed from
within the self to the extent of man's capacity. Through
such revelation, to become the bearer of human rather than
personal pain; of human rather than personal vision; to the
extent, also, that through such revelation man "joins ranks
in the struggle for man's ultimate end—to walk alone as
God's firstborn without mediating angel." Israel alone has
known it even in the figure of Elijah, the so-called prophet
of vengeance who, together with Shoham, prays for Israel:
"God of Mercy, remove the ever-present cup of venom!
. . . Lest thy people shrink back, lest its vision be extin-
guished by cataracts of blood and horror! Out of the mists
of their banishment, their last prayer will inaudibly whisper
to you their longing for the kingdom of the Almighty upon
the earth, their yearning for redemption—redemption for
them and their tormentors. . . ."

Surely, to take another illustration, no reader of Yitzhak
Lamdan will accuse him of self-coddling, of any tendency
to explain away Jewish misery by means of self-flattery, no
matter how lofty, no matter how philosophically subtle.
Hence, the greater significance of the selections to be quoted
from his "For the Sun Declined," a monologue delivered
by Jacob as he flees from Esau to Padan-Aram and lays him-

self to sleep on "some stones of the place," as the Bible puts
it, only to discover in his dream that "it is none other than
the house of God, and this is the gate of heaven." The
poem is further based upon a midrashic parable in which
God "caused the sun to set prematurely, so as to speak to
Jacob in intimate privacy. It is as though a loving friend
came to visit the king from time to time and the king said:
Put out the candles, put out the lanterns, for I wish to speak
to my friend secretly." Now Jacob, according to Lamdan,
soliloquizes as follows:

> Where am I, O awesome friend? Darkness has hedged
>   me in.
> Neither light of heaven, nor earthly lantern, alas!
> It seems that once again you have some love-matter
>   to impart to me,
> And it is too fearful to be spoken within anyone's
>   hearing but mine;
> And it is too precious to be revealed by the light
>   of the daily sun—
> Hence, once again, you cast upon me loneliness and
>   darkness.
>
> Once again, it seems, you call me to share Thy secret—
> So very ponderous, and sublime, divine. . . .
> That is why you have extinguished everything, to conceal
>   my coming and going;
> That is why your hand stretched at my feet a web of
>   horrors,
> And night erects its screen of fears about me—
> That we may not be seen, holding secret council. . . .

Unlike Shoham, Lamdan rebels against this special divine
love of Jacob which must bring night upon him prema-

turely, whenever God seeks to work out his secret plans
with him for "the ultimate good of man." It is not difficult
to hear the echoes of our own times in Jacob's protests
against such special favors:

See, the least road-marker has been wiped off my way!
Not a candle flickering anywhere, not a faint glimmer
    in a lattice.
Thou hast plucked me out of the heart of the world,
    away from all its hues and tinges,
So that I be yours alone, and only with you, with you!
Let me be! I will not be dragged perforce any more
To the gallows of thy love, O Lover and Seducer!
As one, the only chosen one, I am called to thee,
And by the time I come—I am misshapen—crippled;
"Jacob, Jacob!" No, I will not come and listen,
And be once more scorned of man, yet beloved of God.

If you have some matter to impart to me, a great and
    precious matter of love—
Stretch it at my feet as a verdant carpet of spring;
Light it up over my head as a blazing morning-rose.
Let its music sing in a myriad voices that all, that
    all, may hear;
Bejewel with it thy stars at night; thy sun by day,
And let the butterflies of all thy world frolic with it.

Otherwise, neither love, thy love, nor the pain it
    spells!
Let me be, that I may move among the least of the world;
Unaware, like all of them, let me walk the roads of life,
A slave to the toil of day, free—to night's rest;
One thread out of many, woven unbeknown,
Into the web of being, both radiant and somber.

If ever an attempt was made to "debunk" the idea of Israel's election, Lamdan has made it here. Yet, can anyone miss the definite impression that protest as he may, he, too —like Jacob himself—is held spellbound by this awe-inspiring dream of Israel as God's most intimate consultant; and that, therefore—noblesse oblige—the consultations God holds with him are held on God's own terms, in total darkness, "away from . . . hues and tinges" of self-intoxicated, self-sufficient light of day. In spite of himself, Lamdan also knows that however "misshapen—crippled" Jacob is by the time he enters God's secret councils, come to the rendezvous he must, for he is called, he alone is called.

It may be rather farfetched to maintain that this is the conscious meaning of the bloody content of Hebrew war literature. With the exception of a few of the poets, it can hardly be maintained that Hebrew writers during the war years had asked explicit philosophic questions concerning the meaning of the catastrophe. However, insofar as the unconscious query hovers over the bulk of war utterance in Hebrew, the only historic—or better, philosophical— answer to it, however unconsciously given, seems to imply the notion of Israel's destiny in the shaping of humanity, in the emergence of human conscience.

There is a simple ballad by Sh. Shalom which should be cited here as a more homely illustration of the significance of this idea to the Jewish folk mind, as conceived in the spirit of Jewish tradition by the Hebrew poet. In this timely ballad, "Rabbi Mendel, the brother of the Rabbi of Ger," together with his Hasidim, stands surrounded by a German firing squad, while other Jewish prisoners, arrayed in long rows, dig the common grave for the condemned rabbi and his adherents.

Rabbi Mendel observes them:
Despair, destitution, the shadow of death,
Have completely quenched the light in their eyes—
Their only awareness is death.
Is there still room for the uplifting of their souls?
Rabbi Mendel is sorrowfully silent.

Then suddenly he cries out, as if swooning with thirst:
"A glass of water, O Jews, a glass of water!
Half my portion in the world to come
To anyone that takes his life in his hands."
But none stirs, not a man responds—
Doom and hopelessness in all eyes.

"A glass of water," Rabbi Mendel cries. "Isn't there
    anyone?"
And ashamed he is to have broken with speech
That silence of desperation and misery
Forever stamped upon them by enslavement.
But look! A prisoner there has broken forth,
Hobbling through the rows of trained gun-barrels.

A mere Jewish tailor he was, a simple pious man,
Running in his chains to the well.
A glass of water he brought, paying in blood.
Rabbi Mendel performed the oblation,
And began the confession to the Creator of all worlds;
"Amen," the endless spaces responded.

And when the cruel lieutenant gave the order to fire,
Rabbi Mendel smiled to the Highest—
For in the realm of ultimate despair there still was
A Jew sanctifying the name of the Deity,
A Jew loving his fellow, and triumphant,
Even in death, over viciousness and evil.

Speaking of the Jew's will-to-be, Zevi Woislavsky observes that the legend of the Eternal Jew, the character which the Christian myth regards as "a strange creature, forever cursed by God and man, is the greatest attempt made by general folk psychology to extricate itself from its own nightmare of the eternal existence of an eternal people." This myth, according to Woislavsky, seems to declare to historic Jewry: "You say that no lethal weapon will avail against you, that death has no power over you, and you are arrogantly proud of it. Yet this very eternity of yours is a curse from which you are incapable of disentangling yourselves. Having lost all sense of the fear of death, you have also lost all sense of true living, of living as a people of greatness and splendor, of victory and defeat. You have lost the rhythmic sense of growth and decomposition, of blossom-time and autumnal withering. The great cosmic process of being to which all species are subject has disgorged you, so that you are cast about like Isaiah's 'abhorred offshoot,' on the outskirts of life, on the dunghill of universal existence."

This blind Jewish urge to hold on however unheroically to life, was frequently castigated in the writings of the Berdichevsky-Brenner school of contemporary Jewish thought. But the writers of the war years place a quite different construction upon this Jewish will-to-be. Wherever the motif occurs in recent writings, it is elevated to a philosophic height which makes of "the living dog" the true aspirant for the position of the "lion" in the scheme of things.

In this connection, the remarkable tale by Asher Barash, "The Jew That Stayed Behind in Toledo," should be summarized fully. The time is the summer of 1942, when Spanish Jewry was given three months to liquidate its affairs and go into exile. The place is Toledo, and the main character is "the Jew that stayed behind," Don José. "Fortuna da Delmego," Barash tells us, "the wife of Don Abraham Senior, the wealthy Superintendent of Taxation in Toledo, had seven brothers; six of them short, stocky, brave and life-loving men, loudly and ostentatiously amassing wealth; while the seventh, Joseph, popularly known as Don José, was the extreme opposite: tall, slender, serene and aristocratic in appearance, sedate of manner and prone to wistfulness. His business was buying and selling ancient manuscripts in various languages—Greek, Latin and Arabic. He also owned some Hebrew manuscripts, most of them poetry and philosophical treatises of the 11th and 12th centuries. The latter, however, he never sold, but read them for the good of his soul, as a sacred matter. He was not a lighthearted person. Unlike his brothers, he eschewed wealth, since wealth, too, is burdensome—it shackles the soul and robs one of the true enjoyment of life. His home was not built in the Jewish quarter, with its congestion, its oppressive heaviness of living, its noise; it was situated high up on a hill in the southern part of Toledo, overlooking a verdant, well-watered dale below, within the Christian part of the city."

Most of his time Don José spent in the garret of his mansion, where, in brass coffers, he kept his books and scrolls. He had his meals by himself, eating with his family only on the Sabbath and holidays. His brother-in-law, Don Abraham, "the mainstay of the state exchequer and the intimate of the Royal Pair," as well as the venerable Rabbi Isaac Abuhav, regarded Don José as easygoing in matters religious. Don Abraham especially doubted "if Don José, mingling with monks and bishops, would hold his own in the coming great test, with rumors spreading that the Royal Pair were planning soon to exile all the Jews from the whole of Spain." Of course, the Jewish court favorite was certain of his other brothers-in-law, "although the latter were plain men, avid for material possessions."

When the storm broke and there was a meeting of the entire clan at the home of this Jewish worthy, Don Abraham proposed that they all take an oath not to renounce their ancestral faith as the price for the right to remain in Spain, and they all assented vociferously. "Only Don José sat silent through the entire session. Not a syllable did he let drop. His manner bespoke some inner revolt." The clan is outraged. One of the children even stealthily spits in Don José's direction, and as he leaves, Don Abraham places his hand on his shoulder and says in an agitated whisper, "I know that you are a man of self-respect, and will not desecrate, God forbid, the name of Israel." To which Don José replies laconically, "I have not yet cleared all my accounts with the God of my fathers," and walks out erect, so that he almost touches the lintel of the door.

Upon his return home, Don José locks himself up in his garret and falls into a peculiar state of reverie, partly phantasmal vision, partly prophetic insight. "Great lucidity as well as crushing sadness commingled in his state of being." In a vision he sees the world spread out before him and, enacted in it, the scene of the banishment with its sadistic debauchery, its humiliation and its deep human sorrow. He sees the ships carrying the refugees, the storms playing havoc with them. Where will they go? Who will admit them? There is no way out. "All the bribes Jews may weigh in gold into the hands of the rulers will not avail. Conversion to Christianity will be of no use; the converts will not be trusted; they will not be wanted. And in his clear vision he draws up the balance sheet of the Jewish community in Spain, the glory of all contemporaneous Jewish communities—and his balance reduces itself to a total in terms of the ancient prophecy [Ezek. 5]: A third will be scattered to the four corners of the earth; a third will die in terrible torture on land or at sea or wherever they are dispersed; and the third that will remain in Spain will, in part, become apostates, and in part wretched mask-wearers." For hours he sits, absorbed in his melancholy musings, and when the trumpet announces midnight, a great and terrible resolution dawns upon him, clothed in the fiery words of the psalmist: "I shall not die, but live!" (Ps. 118:17). The rest was unimportant: all the passion, all the terror, all of the soul's crying, found their full satisfaction in those words of the psalm. He hurriedly wrote them out on a piece of parchment, and placed the writing (amulet-like) upon his heart, beneath his clothes. Rising in the morning, he left the room where he had stayed in a state of fast, and spoke to his wife the incisive words: "I shall not die."

It is necessary to break up the continuity of the story in order to point out that of the entire verse in the psalm from which Don José picks the writing for his amulet, he uses the first part only. The rest of the verse, "so that I may continue recounting the deeds of God," which explains the psalmist's urge to defy death, does not interest him. His determination to survive is an end in itself, an absolute that requires no philosophical explanation: "My will," he says, "is granite. I shall not die, but live. Any attempt made upon me will not succeed. . . ."

It is hard to say what the consequences of this adamant

will-to-be would have been had Barash sought to read rational meaning into Don José's determination. It must have
been, however, the author's ingenious intent to show that
such irrational determination becomes symbolic, becomes
one of the cardinal principles of Jewish survival just because it is irrational, irreducible, elemental. The exile takes
place. All those who had so nobly taken the oath of allegiance to their ancestral faith at the home of Don Senior become converts to Catholicism, as perhaps might have been
expected. The only one that does not is Don José, and on
the eve of the ninth of Ab, the date of the banishment, he
sets out for the home of one of his friends, a Spanish gran-
dee, whom he wants to present with a precious manuscript,
"as his last gift before leaving Spain." Then the cruelly un-
predictable intervenes to lend greater credence to Don José's
conviction that he is indestructible. On the way to his
friend's palace, he is seized by some Christian youths, who
beat him, rob him of the keys of his treasured coffers and
then turn him over to the Inquisition. There he is kept for
seven days and then put on the wheel. While his body
writhes in hellish pain, he hears only one voice whispering
in him: "I shall not die, I shall not die." When permitted
to go, he drags his mutilated self to his home, helped toward
evening by an old man who risks his life to give him aid
under cover of darkness. His home is brightly illuminated;
his wife and children have already been evicted, and his
monstrous heirs celebrate their orgiastic housewarming.
Half-crazed by the pain of his broken frame, Don José celebrates his own victory over death. "If he could stand up,"
Barash says, "he would rise and dance beneath this lofty sky
studded with stars, with a big moon in their midst. He
would dance there by the roadside in front of his home oc-

cupied by strangers, by cruel fiends, and he would dance the
dance of life, of life forever."

Whether Barash intended it or not, his realism here
sublimates itself into a strange symbolism. For is not Don
José the sublime symbol of Israel, Israel repeatedly too
crippled with physical injury and pain to dance outwardly
"the dance of life, of life forever," which its spirit has
made its own? Of course, such grit, such obstinate clinging
to life, must seem irrational to the inimical onlooker, must
seem mad to the non-Jewish spectator. And because all
Toledo is certain that he is mad, he is finally allowed to
stray at large through the city streets; the passersby even
offer him fruit and crumbs of food. The mob no longer as-
sails him—the Spaniards are very careful not to lay hands
upon "those smitten by God."

Barash does not reveal to the reader whether or not Don
José is insane. Winding up his story he merely concentrates upon the two passions that still feed his hero's flickering life. And these passions, too, assume symbolic meaning,
as the reader follows the author's effortless account of them.
One is Don José's surviving passion for manuscripts, for
every shred of written parchment which he carefully picks
up from the pavement in his endless wandering through the
streets of Toledo, carefully placing them in the sack which
he carries on his back. His other passion is for festive state
and religious processions, which he always follows, mutter-
ing to himself: "I shall not die, I shall not die, but live."
Pageant after pageant, parade after parade—Don José par-
ticipates in every one. The years pass, 1498, 1504, 1509,
1516—historic events unfold in a steady march, but Don
José lives on and follows them all. Then, in the spring of
1540, Philip, still a boy, and destined to revive the horrors

of the Inquisition in Spain and beyond, is proclaimed heir to the throne. Don José is there to witness this ceremony, too, and though in the course of it he finally dies, his passing itself seems to immortalize the fear of eternal Jewish persistence which haunts so much of non-Jewish civilization. Here is the conclusion of the tale in Barash's own words. "Don José, who was then about ninety, saw a great procession of celebrants, and, straightening the sack on his back, marched behind them, alone in the middle of the road. He did not know that it was only the vanguard of the parade, and that the troops of the Infante would come next. Suddenly he heard the hoofs of a neighing horse quickly approaching from behind, and while he sought to turn aside to the edge of the wide open road he was thrown to the ground and the heavily knobbed horseshoes passed over him. He was dazed. In a fiery flash, the words loomed in his brain: 'I shall not die. . . .' But their repetitious continuity dimmed, for his soul departed. The horse of the Infante, the boy Philip, had trampled him to death. A crowd gathered about the dead old man. The amulet was found. Philip ordered his tutor to read the writing, but he could not, for it was the unfamiliar script of the Hebrews. The boy was angered and swore at him. It is said that on that day the evil spirit rested upon Philip, which did not release its hold on him for the rest of his life, and upon his death it became the heritage of the people of Spain to this very day."

The story must be read in its entirety if one is to discover for oneself all the rich allusions to Jewish history, past and present, with which the author endows the figure of Don José, that vivid if somewhat uncanny symbol of the eternal Jew, who just refuses to cease being. He is the symbol of

the Jew's indomitable clinging to life as he follows the continued pageant of world history, sure that the ultimate
meaning of that pageant he alone correctly reads in the
pieces of parchment which he stores in his wanderer's sack.

Only in our own day has the historic Jewish will-to-be
assumed concrete expression in the form of the Palestinian
effort. Palestine, as the last-ditch stand made by Jewry in
its desperate struggle for survival, is not a new theme in
contemporary Hebrew letters. Yitzhak Lamdan's "Masada"
has for twenty-five years been the most personal poetical
expression of the yearnings, both human and Jewish, of
hundreds of thousands of young Jews training as Halutzim
the world over; and the central idea of "Masada" is this
awareness on the part of the young Jewish pioneer that in
the land of Israel the Jew fights the final battle for Jewry,
for Jewish historicity. But who are, who have been these
hundreds of thousands of Halutzim who are in their deepest
significance depicted here by the poet? Lamdan portrays the
most representative types setting out for "Masada," the last
Jewish fortress, i.e., Palestine, in the several monologues
at the opening of his poem, in which each of the protagonists introduces himself.

These *dramatis personae* of the Halutz movement are not
starry-eyed romanticists, naïve dreamers, or fanatics. They
are forlorn young Jews on the brink of Jewish despair,
which you find so amply represented on every American college campus, in every American social movement. They are
just unhappy, forlorn Jews; unable to continue as Jews,
unable to disappear as Jews. They are Lamdan's candidates
for Masada. Some are the Jewish nihilists who know that
"there is no way out." But, intellectually, one course is open
to them—to avenge themselves upon the cruel world, to
pour their despair into the blood of the world, so that the

world revolution which they preach may be "the knife that must be driven into the belly of a world swollen with gorging itself upon our flesh." Others, while also crying that Masada is utter falsehood, a mere will-o'-the-wisp in the dark of universal night, honestly crave the world revolution as the means of doing away with the "Jewish problem" as it is called, or in the poet's words, "to pass arm-in-arm on with a tortured, pining world into the kingdom of the all-atoning love." Still others, also scoffing at Masada, are the disillusioned intellectuals, they who abandon all effort to save Israel, to save the world for that matter, since everything in the nature of social effort is so boring, so uselessly boring, that self-indulgence, especially toying with every kind of philosophical and artistic doctrine is by far the wiser way, till the whole world explodes into nothingness. That is the stuff the young Jew is made of as he scoffs at Masada, before he joins the ranks of those who fight for Masada—the land of Israel.

Somehow they have come to Palestine, somehow they have been coming for the last thirty or forty years, and even while in Palestine, many of them are merely "workers, watchmen, poets, some naive souls, others just adventurers," as David Shimonovitz describes them in his idyll "Dewdrops at Night," which traces the history of pioneering in Palestine in the course of the past forty years. Many of them did not even stay on, "but departed, went away, peeved and disillusioned"; many more "have aged prematurely, and their spirit, too, has aged." How, then, has the miracle happened? How has pioneering Eretz Israel come to prove to the world, to friend and foe alike, that this effort at re-creating Jewish history is not the empty dream it was thought to be only a short time ago by both foe and friend? The answer is given with added force by much of the litera-

ture produced in Palestine during the war, that part of it
especially which is the story not of the historical Jewish
gravitation toward the restoration, but of the restoration itself; the story, in fictional form, most of it, of the draining
of swampland and the establishment of flourishing settlements in malaria-ridden regions; of warding off constant
danger, climatic and human; of living and dying in the process; the story, also, of the recapture of poise, dignity and
self-confidence by the Jew through physical work which
replants him, as it were, in the realness of being.

As he observes his Palestinian-born son, the hero of
"Dewdrops at Night" is at times given to soul-searing
doubt as to the ultimate meaning of this new rootage which
he, like tens of thousands of his fellows, has attempted on
behalf of historic Jewry. To quote a revealing passage:

> Perhaps—may I not be sinful saying it—these free-
>   born children of the Revival
> Are poorer and lowlier in soul than the dry-drained
>   children of the Diaspora.
> They lack the depth achieved by children of affliction
>   only,
> The radiant yearnings known only to those that dwell
>   in the dark,
> The longings for redemption with which none can com-
>   pare for wistful mellowness,
> Which have nurtured countless generations in the
>   heroism of martyrdom—
> In the aspiration for sanctity and purity, and for
>   something lofty in living. . . .
> They are too superficial and lightminded, their
>   spiritual horizons how narrow. . . .

Thus one mood of the Jew that dwells in Zion when questioning the very ultimates of Zion redeemed.

But as against such questions and doubts the musing continues a moment later in quite the opposite direction:

> Is not this boy, hunched at the hoofs of the cow
>   he milks,
> Scrubbing the walls of the hen-house and weeding
>   the garden,
> Carrying on his tender shoulders the full pails,
> Pecking with the hoe the obdurate rocky soil;
> He who knows by name all the weeds and flowers of
>   the village,
> Who without fear wanders about in the mountains
>   and explores their caves,
> To whom every clod and bush of his native village
>   is a friend—
> Is he not the scion of the tree of stout-hearted
>   Hebrews,
> They who knew how to love their little land,
>   ever beset,
> As if gripped with pincers, by mighty, violent
>   neighbors,
> They who knew how to defend their native soil
>   so heroically—
> Those threshers of wheat, those drovers, and
>   dressers of sycamores,
> Who have given saviors and prophets to the world?

Saviors and prophets to the world these honest toilers may yet beget—that is the silent hope behind the dogged penurious effort made by the Palestinian pioneer as Pales-

tinian literature sees him. It is an unspoken faith—for there
are few literatures that innerly fear the grandiloquent as
does the Palestinian. It is of the real, the obviously human,
that this literature speaks even in moments of most fervent
conviction.

Yet even during the war the larger implication of that
effort has not been forgotten. To quote again David Shimonovitz who addresses himself to the builders of Jewish
history in Palestine:

> I do remember all the weight and loftiness of the
>   mission
> Which Providence has thrust upon you, sons and
>   brothers;
> You are to weld together the eternal bridge broken
>   asunder—half of its foundations in the past,
> The other half in the mists of the future, but the
>   wrenched arches
> Suspended limply over the tide, the surging tide
>   of the present
> That storms and ravenously seeks to swallow them,
>   overthrowing the very foundations.
> You are to weld together—with elemental effort—
>   the eternal bridge ripped apart,
> And extricate with superhuman toil, and set moving
>   along the broad highway
> The Chariot of Redemption trapped in the wreckage. . . .

The formula is still the same: It is Redemption that Jewish
historicity leads to; but the continued functioning of that
historicity is impossible unless the people returns to itself.
But the return is painful.

CHAPTER X

Religious Motifs
in Modern Hebrew Poetry

IT IS commonly assumed that modern Hebrew poetry is almost exclusively secular. Yet nothing could be farther from the truth than this popular notion which even the student of Hebrew literature tends to share with the average reader. Neither of them is to be blamed for this, for the historians and critics themselves have developed this view of the nonreligious character of Hebrew literature so successfully that it may take decades to correct their error and place the so-called secularism of this literature within its legitimate bounds.

There are several reasons for this distorted perspective, one of the most obvious being the essentially humanistic character of modern Hebrew literature. In the whole two hundred years of its development it has recorded Jewish aspirations for a richer life on earth, for greater satisfaction in all phases of worldly existence: political and economic, social and cultural. It is, therefore, natural that more prominent leitmotifs of this literature should be those which sound the yearnings for the humanization of Jewish life, for that aspect of human existence which is generally regarded as "worldly" or "secular." But, while Hebrew literature reflects most sympathetically the Jew's growth and development in the generally human sense, it is also preoccupied with the problem of Jewish historical continuation.

In the last seventy-five years especially the literature has pondered one paramount question: How can the Jew continue *qua* Jew while all his energies are bent upon the normalization of his human existence, with the consequent disintegration of those folk patterns which have molded his distinct group identity in the protracted history of Jewish medievalism? As it grapples with this problem of Jewish survival, Hebrew literature in recent generations strives to register its love for the uniqueness and nobility of the passing world of the ghetto. In poem, story and essay, it almost consciously seeks to preserve for posterity its awareness of the greatness of Jewish tradition. It idealizes the Jew as the bearer of the God-idea. It portrays Jewish piety and saintliness. It sings Jewish love of Torah. It even glories in the concept of the Jewish mission in human history. In short, it becomes a veritable museum of the beauty that was traditional Judaism.

Thus, upon careful examination, modern Hebrew literature of necessity proves to be a treasury of Jewish loyalties of a truly religious character which the historian and the philosopher of these letters should long ago have come to note and to interpret. Yet such has been the pressure of outer circumstances upon Jewish life in the past seventy-five years, that historians of Hebrew letters have tended to concentrate upon the more timely and transitory humanistic features of the literature and overlook almost entirely the more permanent, more deeply-rooted Jewish loyalties in which this literature abounds. For all the religious fervor, for instance, which modern Hebrew literature has read into Zionism and the achievements of Halutziut it is diffi-

cult to find a single study of Palestinian letters which
treats of the nature and implications of this fundamental
faith. The critics repeatedly have discussed the political,
social and even economic trends in the literature depicting
Halutziut. But they have failed to note the endless number
of lyrics, ballads and dramatic poems whose explicit subject matter is rugged Halutziut, but whose implicit motiva-
tion is the watchful waiting for the God-sent Messiah. We
find the two commingling even in the following homespun
verses by one of the minor poets of Palestine, Abraham
Braudes:

> I know how to walk behind camels in the sands,
> How to carry upon my back a heavy hump of afflictions,
> And look out for the Messiah.
> And I also know how to stand among the many
>   in the hollow in a quarry,
> How to cleave the rock primeval,
> And look out for the Messiah.

Hebrew criticism in recent years has undoubtedly been
struck by the fervent strain, bordering on the religious, in
the new poetry of the land of Israel. In the spirit of A. D.
Gordon, the critics have even used the term "religion of
labor" to characterize the ultimate meaning of Halutziut
in Palestinian poetry. But they have not yet seriously attempted to tap the welling sources of religion in the poetry
even while speaking of the "religion of labor" which inspires it. If religion has any meaning at all, it means, and has
always meant, three things at least: the consciousness of an
entity greater than self; the longing to merge one's self
with that greater entity; and the peculiar conviction that
such merging foreshadows the millennium, the triumph of

the Good in the world, or the establishment of the Kingdom of Heaven on earth. Palestinian poetry, *in toto,* manifests these three characteristics so markedly that critics in
recent years have often been impelled to admit a dim consciousness of their presence there. Yet that consciousness
remains dim at best. In general, the critics prefer to speak
of the "more rational" elements of social significance inherent in Halutz poetry—of the humanizing effect of labor
upon the Halutz, of the ethical element in collective living,
of the self-consecration on the part of the pioneer to the
service of Jewry. But the student of this poetry remains
blind to the less rational inspiration of that poetry, to the
definitely religious ecstasy which it often exhibits.

It was A. M. Habermann who was the first to publish an
anthology of Hebrew religious poetry to include material
from the last hundred years, his "Liturgical Poems, Ancient
and Modern." The book contains the best traditional liturgical poetry in Hebrew produced in many different lands
over a period of one thousand years at least, beginning with
the work of the Palestinian Jose ben Jose in the 6th century
C.E. and ending with the work of the Yemenite Shalom
Shabasi, who died in the 17th century. But Habermann's
collection is remarkable for quite another reason. He is the
first to have realized the intimate relationship between the
religious poetry to be found in modern Hebrew literature
and that of the earlier periods. He is a path-blazer in linking some of the religious—more strictly speaking, synagogal—moods in modern Hebrew poetry to similar moods
in the work of the time-honored liturgists of Judaism. A
mere glance at the index convinces one of the legitimacy of
the relationship. There you will find the name of Hayyim
Nahman Bialik following that of Rabbi Bahya ben Joseph

(1040–1090); that of Abraham Braudes followed by Rabbi Baruch ben Samuel of Mayence (d. 1221); the American-born Reuben Grossman alphabetically preceding Rabbi Gershom Meor ha-Golah (d. 1028); Jacob Cohen next to Israel Najara (16th century); and the sainted thinker and mystic, Hillel Zeitlin, next to a list of the so-called anonymous poets of early medieval centuries. Not that Habermann's selections from the modern period are the best possible, or that they fully represent all the varieties of religious experience in modern Hebrew poetry. Quite the contrary is true; for it was Habermann's intention to include only poems which are liturgical—actual or potential prayers which may be incorporated in the synagogal service—while the religious theme in modern Hebrew poetry presents many variations of a metaphysical, mystic, ethical and social content. This anthology, however, may prove a turning point in the history of modern Hebraic letters in that it points the way to the discovery of the sacred theme in the Hebrew poetry of recent generations.

Before examining the theme of "groping toward God" in Palestinian poetry especially, it might be well to consider some of its more universal moods in modern Hebrew poetry generally, as it treats of the personal and transcendental God; the immanent God; and the God of modern atomized man. Surprisingly enough much of the religious poetry in modern Hebrew still harks back to the uniquely Jewish notion of God, author of all being, whose purpose in creating the world was purely anthropocentric—namely, that man might recognize the glory of Him by whose will all came to be. In its most elementary statement it is reminiscent of all we know in sacred Hebrew poetry, beginning with "The heavens declare the glory of God," and on to Judah

ha-Levi's "Setting forth toward You, I find you confronting me." A good example of this are the lines by Joseph
Zevi Rimmon:

> God lives! the luminousness of the sky declares it,
> And the stormy black that wraps the sky bespeaks it.
> God lives! the adornment of the earth declares it,
> And the pluck of trees in the tornado bespeaks it;
> God lives! the day in its gold declares it,
> And the night with its terrors bespeaks it;
> God lives! translucent rivers declare it,
> And the heavily weighing fog bespeaks it;
> God lives! the overgrown mountains declare it,
> And the turbulent fires within them bespeak it;
> God lives! life in its springtide declares it,
> And cruel death bespeaks it;
> God lives! the sea with its wrathful waves declares it,
> And in its mutest wistfulness bespeaks it;
> God lives! my strange heart tossing declares it,
> And pouring itself out into God's lap bespeaks it.

The stark simplicity of these lines is not entirely characteristic of modern Hebrew poetry in its celebration of the
personal and transcendental God. It is not even characteristic of Rimmon himself in many other similarly ecstatic
religious moods. The monolithic faith in the existence of
God, as one finds it not only in the Psalms or Job but in
Solomon ibn Gabirol or Judah ha-Levi, is not the permanent mood of the modern Hebrew poet. His religious feeling is for the most part but one of the many tensions which
constitute his poetic world. Yet therein perhaps lies his
chief attraction for the modern reader who also tends to
set out in quest of God rather than to discover, in the words

of ha-Levi, that he always finds himself confronted by God without seeking him.

It should also be pointed out that Rimmon is one of the most religious poets in modern Hebrew literature, a poet with whom the totality of human experience directly sublimates itself and is unconsciously transmuted into an intimate contact, a permanent relationship, with God. It is important therefore to remember that this transcendental aspect of the personal God frequently inspires many modern Hebrew poets whose ambient air may scarcely be said to be constantly charged with a sense of the ever-present God. Few Hebrew readers would spontaneously think of Bialik as a religious poet. Of course, we all know that Bialik, crowned the national Hebrew poet, was the mouthpiece of Jewish suffering and despair as well as of Jewish grit and tenacity, of Jewish inveterate faith in the indestructibility of the Jew's will-to-be. Yet, few among us realize Bialik's abiding clinging to the God of his fathers, in the most traditional sense of the phrase. It would take us too far afield to analyze the idea of God in Bialik's poetry. Actually, this has already been done by Isaac Rivkind in an excellent study, entitled "The God of Bialik." The following passage from Bialik exemplifies his concept:

> Thy breath, O God! flitted by me and I was scorched,
> Thy fingertip, one little moment, made my heartstrings
> tremulous,
> And there I crawled mute, and held in check the
> surging of my spirit;
> My heart swooned within me, and my inner music
> could not billow forth;
> Wherewith dare I enter the sanctuary, and how can
> my prayer be pure,

> While my language, O God! has become defiled, is
>   all uncleanliness,
> Not a word therein but is besmirched down to its
>   root,
> Not a phrase but filthy lips have befouled,
> Not a thought but has been dragged to the house
>   of shame? . . .
> Where can I remove myself from this smell?
> O, where can I hide from this empty tumult?
> Where is the Seraph to cleanse my mouth with his
>   fiery coal?
> I will go forth to the birds of the field that
>   chirp at dawn,
> Or arise and go now to the children playing by
>   the gate;
> I will go and mingle with them in their multitude,
>   will learn their speech and their chatter—
> Will be purified by their breath, and wash my lips
>   with their cleanliness. . . .

Such lines of Bialik's register the impact upon him of the God-idea in terms reminiscent of prophecy and biblical hymnology and the prayer book, and suggest their appropriateness for inclusion in the modern prayer book, with but minor adaptations here and there. Rereading Bialik's collected works with this in view, one must agree with Rivkind: " . . . the God of Israel is Bialik's God. . . . At times he grovels before him; at times he nestles up to him self-pamperingly as does a child to his father; he sometimes even rebels against him, but his rebellion does not endure. . . . Nor is the mention of God with him a mere euphemism, a question of 'form' only. Nor is it because

Bialik initiated the so-called 'prophetic style' in Hebrew poetry, the manner of the prophet who, of course, always speaks in the name of God. It is rather because with Bialik the God of Israel is the God of eternity, the absolute Infinite, the cause of all causes, and the source of all being. . . . There are no metaphysical problems in Bialik. . . . Existentially, the Deity, like nature itself . . . is not even to be questioned. For (in midrashic phrasing) the palace cannot exist without the assumption of a 'leader' (dwelling in the palace); the universe cannot exist without its helmsman. In the spirit of choice Aggadah, Bialik achieved his awareness of the Creator of man and the Fashioner of the universe."

Unfortunately there is not sufficient space for further discussion of Bialik's God-inspired world in all its ramifications, in the poet's attitudes to nature, love, human sorrow and the tragic grandeur of Israel. Nor is there space to analyze further the ever-present awareness of the personal God in the work of Bialik's contemporaries and successors in modern Hebrew poetry. One illustration, however, may perhaps be cited from the work of another poet, Jacob Cohen, a romantic lyricist whose treatment of love, landscape and pantheist yearning for union with eternity is generally universalistic, with but little in his work suggestive of the traditionally Judaic. His Jewishness is predominantly modern Jewish nationalism with its refusal to accept the Jew's orphanhood in the world and its insistence upon the conscious precipitation of the arrival of messianic redemption. Even his lengthy dramatizations of the legendary elements in the lives of David and Solomon are not specifically pious. And yet, he is the author of a great number of lyrics which could easily be grouped into a homogeneous collection of odes and hymns almost synagogal in nature. Here are a few lines from a short poem of his entitled "The Face of God":

Out of the deepest depths of the wells of my soul,
To thee, O hiding God! I cry—hearken my prayer:
Demand whatever thou wilt of me, O God! Behold I
   am ready,
But show me thy face, only show me thy face!
Of what avail the splendor of all the worlds thou
   hast planted in my heart?
They are but pallid shadows of thy treasured light,
Mere vague lineaments of thine own image.
Yet, I thirst to drink from the source of all
   sources,
I long to steep myself in the light of light—
Thy face, *thy* face I crave to see.
"Man shall not see my face and live!"—Be it so
Indeed, let me die this very great moment,
Once I have seen thy face, O high and exalted God!
Lord, light up all thy light for me one moment—
And mothlike I will plunge into it, and be utterly
   consumed.

This aspect of the God-idea in modern Hebrew poetry is closely related to that intoxication with nature which has literally overwhelmed the Hebrew muse in recent generations. The starved denizen of the gloomy ghetto; the ascetic who for centuries had denied himself all sensory enjoyment of the physical universe; the scholar and mystic who for many generations had dreaded the seductive beauty of the tree and the ploughed field because such beauty might tempt him from study or meditation and jeopardize his life eternal—all these seem to have found release in the burst of nature-poetry in modern Hebraic creativity. It is difficult to think of a contemporary literature in any other language since the Romantic Age, since the days of young Goethe, Chateaubriand, Wordsworth, Keats and Shelley, in which the adoration of nature looms as large as it has in the modern Hebrew in the past fifty years. Indeed, in its wholehearted absorption in the unending pageantry of earth and sky, of mountain and field and river, of night and day and all the seasons of the year, modern Hebrew literature can best be compared with some literature of the European Renaissance, the Elizabethan, for instance. Yet, paradoxically perhaps, Hebrew nature-poetry seldom if ever becomes strictly pagan. It seldom celebrates a landscape or any natural object as an end in itself. However sweeping the reaction to nature, however sensitive the self-consecration to sense impressions, those impressions are always suffused with the awareness of the ever creative force of life. Even Saul Tchernichovsky may scarcely be regarded as an exception to this rule. As a poet he literally worships the might and beauty of nature in terms often strikingly pagan and even celebrates the gods of the ancient and classical worlds. Yet his rich song of field and forest also appears to grope for some all-embracing principle of religious worship. His adoration of ever creative cosmic nature approaches a mystic conception of some divine spirit vitalizing universal existence. Tchernichovsky's nature-poetry, abundant, sturdy yet throbbing, is best characterized in these two lines of his:

> Wherever there is an awareness of life in the
>   flesh and blood,
> There He invests himself in the plant, in the clod.

The psalmist's cry, "God, how multifarious are thy works," should perhaps be paraphrased in application to Tchernichovsky, in terms pantheistic, "God, how multifarious art thou in thy works." But the impulsion toward the constant rediscovery of God in nature is for the most part shared by Tchernichovsky with the rest of modern Hebrew poets.

In his nature-poetry, the Hebrew poet is of course less intent upon stressing the God-idea than upon indulging his pictorial sense of the marvels of the visible universe. It is not often that he subordinates nature to the indwelling God of nature, as Joseph Zevi Rimmon does in the following verses:

> How may I sing of day and night—
> It is God who molded them.
> How may I sing of heaven and earth—
> It is God who founded them.
> How may I sing of mountains and hills—
> It is God who planted them.
> How may I sing of seas and deserts—
> It is God who begot them.
> How may I sing of the world and its plenitude—
> It is God who bade them be.
> I shall sing to him who fashioned all and is
>   exalted above all—
> It is to God I must sing.

Generally, the sense of God is secondary to the poet's fusion with the natural scene, as we find it in the following short lyric by Judah Karni:

> Night is sublime, its moon-dominated dome
>   Is so powerful, yet ever so gentle.

Night ripens clusters of stars,
  None of them fall, nor are quenched.
Night is heightened and deep, yet serene,
  None binds the sacrifice, none is bound.
Night equates elevation with decline,
  It is immaculate.
Night articulates for the amazed and perplexed.
  O Lord! O God!

The implications of pantheism in poetry are well known to readers of English and American 19th century literature. In modern Hebrew poetry, it would seem even pantheism is Judaized, so that it often becomes difficult to mark it off from the more normative conception of the transcendental God of prophetic Judaism. In the first place, pantheistic Hebrew poetry tends to point directly to the indwelling spirit of nature as God rather than to leave the reader with the mere awareness of that indwelling spirit as some anonymous cosmic force. In that respect it is more reminiscent of the work of Gerard Manley Hopkins than of Emerson or even of Tennyson.

Secondly, and perhaps more important, modern Hebrew pantheism seldom quite forgets the *ethical* implications of the conception of the cosmic spirit inherent in all existence. If it is God that impels all nature to everlasting efflorescence, it is also God who in man's heart craves for the Good —for love and justice and the self-perfection of human life. In one of his well-known radical works, "The Visions of the False Prophets," Tchernichovsky expresses this idea almost programmatically for all of modern Hebrew literature. In the first three poems, he makes one of these presumed false prophets utter his protests against the evisceration, the over-spiritualization of Jewish life resulting from

what he regards as petrified rabbinic Judaism. He also sets
forth his ideals of the new Jew—the wholesome human
being who loves life rather than fears its so-called tempta-
tions, who seeks to make of the earth the paradise-on-earth
for man as individual as well as social being. But the very
poem which celebrates the new Jew as natural man contrasted with the fear-ridden ascetic of the ghetto ends with
a short lyric which should be summarized here for its
strange reversion to the idea of God, once again insisting
on the duties of the human heart through which he manifests himself even as he, in nature, insists, as it were, on
manifesting himself through mere biological being:

> If you ask me concerning God, my God:
> "Where is he that we may worship him with resonant
>   song?"
> Here on earth, too, he is: the heavens are not
>   for him—
> But the earth he has given to man.
>
> The beautiful tree, the beautiful plough-land—
>   therein also the likeness of his image;
> Upon every mountainside he plays hide and seek;
> Wherever there is an awareness of life in the
>   flesh and blood,
> There he invests himself in the plant, in the clod.
>
> His next of kin—all that is: the doe, the turtle,
> The scrawny bush and the dark cloud pregnant with
>   thunder;
> For he is not the God of would-be spirits—he is
>   the God of the human heart:
> That is his name and that is his memorial to all
>   eternity.

Thus, even the most pantheistic of modern Hebrew poets is driven back not only to subsuming all of nature under the conception of God but also to the conception of the human heart as all-significant in his pantheism. It is man's heart that registers the oneness of all existence; but it is man's heart also, in this poem, that out of its sense of the oneness of life must proceed to build a free and noble human world based upon the old biblical principles of love and justice and the ennoblement of human existence.

Yet the most remarkable manifestation of the tenacious hold of the God-idea upon modern Hebrew poetry is to be found in the work of the post-Bialik generation—in the work of men and women who have sung the bewilderment and forlornness of the so-called wasteland in which all mankind has been wandering for the last thirty years. This wasteland is no characteristic of Hebrew literature alone. The term has been adopted from the title of a poem by T. S. Eliot, and well applies to the mood of the best of European and American literature of the past three decades whose protagonist is the disillusioned contemporary, the modern intellectual left with nothing but corroding self-questioning. It is this modern intellectual whom one is sometimes tempted to call atomized man insofar as his reflection in contemporary literature is concerned. The Atomic Age has arrived but recently upon the political scene. But upon the literary scene, the atomic age has stamped itself indelibly for the past thirty years. Thomas Mann in the German novel, Marcel Proust in the French, James Joyce in the English, and Thomas Wolfe in the American, all have depicted modern man's conscious life as a series of atomized moments—agonized moments seeking to achieve a sense of unity, of goal and purpose, but remaining doomed to an

awareness of bewildering disunity, to an anguishing search
for time ever lost, ever purposeless. The poetry of the age,
in all languages, offers the same portrayal of modern man
lost in the unending frustration of atomized moments that
will not constitute a unity, that cannot produce a formula
spelling philosophic continuity of human endeavor and
aspiration. And Hebrew poetry, also, to the extent that it
mirrors the life of the individual soul, is no stranger to this
forlorn search for the meaning of life, for some principle
of continuity and goal, save in the social sense. The moment
rather than eternity, therefore, reigns supreme in the experiential content of much of the Hebrew poetry of the
last three decades.

It is thus highly significant to note the unconscious turning to God of even the anguished, warped moment of experience; as, for instance, the prayerful mood in the works
of Mordecai Temkin, collected recently under the general
title of "Songs and Prayers":

> I am ashamed, my God, of my flesh
> That is slowly decaying
> Without knowing any more
> How to perform thy exalted bidding.
> I am ashamed that like a dog, old
> And deaf,
> And stretched on his paws
> I do not speedily arise
> At the sound of thy chiding, my God!

or:

> Forgive me, my God,
> That like muddy water

I have poured out my life
Upon the earth.
Forgive me that all my bruises
Are selfmade;
And yet, weeping like a beaten child,
I have cried to you
That you bandage my bruises, O God!

or:

Melancholy is the host of my days upon the earth.
You have raised a rampart about me,
And segregated me from all mankind.
My hands
That have lusted to take all
You have folded in silence
That I look upon the world
Like a transient.
And you, God, also have become to me
Like wine to one embittered of heart.
Yet wine unpoured.

This sense of utter helplessness is sometimes changed
into a sense of the triumphant worth of the moment which
seems to prognosticate the ultimate achievement of meaning. But this mood, again, ultimately formulates itself into
a conviction, however vague, that the fragmentation of experience is but a test of man's capacity to hammer out a
philosophy of life. Yet who is it that tests man's capacity?
Who is it that brings modern man to trial? The answer often
is God, as in the following lines by Uri Zevi Greenberg:

Like chapters of prophecy my days burn in all
    their revelation,

And my body in their midst is like the thick lump
    of metal intended for smelting.
And over me stands my God, the blacksmith, and
    strikes with all might:
Each wound cut in me by time opens a lesion,
And casts forth the imprisoned flame in sparks of
    moments.
This is my sentence and destiny till evening on the
    road.
And when I return to thrust the smitten lump of my
    body upon the bed,
My mouth is an open wound.
All naked I then speak with my God: You have worked
    hard,
Now night has come; desist—let us both rest.

The mood of the wanderer in the modern wasteland, so
rare in modern literature, is a permanent feature in contemporary Hebrew poetry. This mood is best suggested by
Jacob Steinberg in a short lyric in which he speaks of himself as "a seafarer whose sail has fallen asleep in the heart
of noon," or as "a weary fisherman in a tiny lifeboat filled
with unrealizable dreams and desires." Hence, Steinberg's
outcry—an actual refrain—in his poem, "Oh, lead me on
yet a while longer, Father in Heaven!" Such poetry frequently resorts to God in its very inability to express concretely its faith in God. Perhaps this is why this kind of
poetry lends itself best to interpretation for modern man
in *his* mute yearning for faith coupled with *his* inability to
express firmly his actual faith in God. Faith in God speaks
out in terms altogether unequivocal only when the modern
Hebrew poet ceases to sing his own personal life and becomes the mouthpiece of Jewish history and Jewish faith.

CHAPTER XI

The Quest for Faith
in Palestinian Literature

WHEN WE turn to the Palestinian expression of personal groping toward God we find that it is even more subdued than the earlier poetry we have quoted. It often seems to be bound by some sort of self-imposed Hippocratic oath in its tacit allegiance to understatement in depicting the fervor, indeed, the quest, for faith which inspires the new Jewish life in Palestine. Rabbi Simha Bunam of Pzhysha, one of the most original figures in the history of Hasidism, when asked by his disciples why he consistently refrained from writing, is known to have replied: "I have always wanted to compose a book, no larger than a quarter of a page, and call it *Man*. But I have bethought myself that it is best to leave even that book unwritten." There is something of the same hesitation with regard to the efficacy of human expression in the tenor of Palestinian letters as they haltingly seek to present the emergence of the new type of Jew, indeed, of the new type of man, in the land of Israel. Humility becomes especially imperative with this literature as it ponders the ultimates of the Jewish revival, as it meditates upon the sublimities of human fate and destiny which it sees inhering, however generally, in the Jewish revival. With Sh. Shalom, Palestinian literature cries out to the veiled future:

> O brother, my brother in ages far distant,
> For you I yearn out of the thick mist.

With him it asserts:

> The battle of God concealed in life is my battle.

But, with him, it remains perplexed as to the clear formulation of the new emergent Jewish relationship to the ultimates: to human fate in the world, to man's share in cosmic destiny, to God. With him, Palestinian literature frequently broods:

> I am lost in new sounds, I am lost in new silences,
> I am lost in the storm ever surging in my abysses. . . .
> What am I? What my life? What my land? My people?
> The Rider of the Infinite wildly prances in my
>   expanses. . . .

It is this peculiar juxtaposition of two kinds of inner knowledge that makes Palestinian literature shun the clearly defined statement of its deepest convictions. On the one hand, it somehow knows that the well-nigh miraculous re-birth of Jewry in its ancestral homeland is the modern manifestation at its most glorious of the Jew's historic battle, "the battle of God concealed in life." On the other hand, the annunciation of this truth is still too overwhelming in its "new sounds" and "new silences" for the literature to profane it by premature definition. Bold abstraction, stark statement of tenets, terrify the Palestinian imagination precisely because the intensity of the new life approximates a religiousness which eludes formulation.

The essence of the group experience in the land of Israel is represented in this literature as practically incommunicable, as a blended emotional and intellectual awareness which cannot be grasped unless lived and registered on the spot, in the land of Israel itself. Unless you have loved you cannot understand the meaning of love. Unless death has stalked across your path you cannot fathom the fear of death. Unless, at some moment of your own life, you have been stirred by the creative impulse, you cannot conceive of the thrill of creativity. Yet, portrayed in literature, the attitude of the pioneer toward the revival of the land, as we have seen, appears compacted of these three elements— a limitless love of land and people, a profound sense of danger threatening Jewry the world over, and an almost supernatural creativity. The resurrection of the wasteland is, perhaps, self-sufficient to the Palestinian Jew: it does not necessarily connote to him the miraculous fulfillment of Hosea's prophecy of the earth that "shall respond to her inhabitants." Reflected, however, in literature, each of the elements entering the group experience shines forth as a facet of traditional Jewish faith.

It would take us too far afield to compare fully the attitudes toward the inherently religious in the covenant between Israel and the land of Israel as they are mirrored in modern Hebrew letters, and in the bulk of traditional Jewish literature. Yet striking examples of a strict parallelism between the new and the old are so abundant that a few at least may be adduced. There is, for instance, the following midrashic passage: "At the very beginning of the creation of the world, the Holy One, blessed be he, engaged first of all in planting; that is the significance of the text: 'And the Lord God planted a garden in Eden.' You, too, when you enter the land, shall engage in planting first." And in ever so many tones and overtones, Palestinian poetry seems to indicate that at long last the Jew, with his return today to a life of "planting" in the land of his fathers, only fulfills the injunction first imposed by God upon himself, as an example for Israel in the future. Here is a lyric, one of many on this theme, by Levi ben Amittai:

Now I know my boundary. The line of the furrow stretches.
Tread on, and crush the multitudinous rocky obstacles,
Though rain pour in torrents, the sun beat down,
The hurricane assail from the threshold of the nearby
    desert.

Listen to the beat of hooves, to the echo of desiccated
    earth,
And see: Our muscles are taut upon the plough.
Upon my back, too, O mule, mute friend,
There is someone to strike with the lash.

Arise and pierce with the plough-knife! Arise and turn
    the clod!
Uncover to the sun the aching flesh of the earth.
O God! When wilt thou appear to pull the harrow
With the fingers of thy hand over the scabs of this
    earth?

Perhaps it will not be stretching parallels too far to hear the same idea in these symbolistic stanzas by Abraham Shlonsky, reminiscent of early pioneering in the plain of Jezreel, some twenty-five years ago:

At night, the tents—great lanterns—are lighted,
And the mountains of Gilboa breathe:
Who is it there meditating black evil,
Like some great gaping beast?

Long-haired Balaam, with eyes wide-open—
Night rides upon a black she-ass;
Yet, the mountains of Gilboa crouch beneath him,
They feel the rustle of God's hand sowing.

With hand all hairy, heaped with stars,
God sows the seed of the Vision.
Black lips tremulously whisper:
How goodly are thy tents, O Jezreel!

In simple lyrics of this kind, charged with human pathos, one cannot fail to discern the reverberations of Israel's yearnings for salvation. Much of Palestinian literature will some day be recognized as the multiple modern restatement of the theme of salvation so central in Jewish traditional lore, in all its aspects—individual, national and universal. Explicitly, it sounds a more modest tune: a home for the homeless, a shelter for the hounded; warmth and comfort for the disowned, the broken and mutilated is its burden. On the surface it frequently tends in quite the opposite direction in its expression of the hopes and aspirations pervading the present-day restoration. In terms of so-called practical Zionism, it frequently reasserts the well-known insistence of that profound though harried champion of a transvaluation of values in Jewish life and history, M. J. Berdichevsky: "Give us a stone upon which to rest our heads. Then we shall dream." Or, in the words of Jacob Steinberg: "We wish to descend downhill where the atmosphere is heavy and a mist rises from the earth, hiding distances from view." Yet even Berdichevsky's outcry for a mere stone upon which to rest Jewish heads does not envisage the humble stone as an end in itself. Alluding to the biblical "stones of the place" that Jacob had gathered before

he lay down to dream of angels ascending and descending
the ladder reaching from earth to heaven, Berdichevsky
also, critical as he is of Jewish indulgence in daydreaming,
knows that with a stone of our own under our heads we shall
dream the eternal dream of Jacob we needs must continue
weaving. Jacob Steinberg, urging the Jewish descent
"downhill," knows that such a Jewish descent is a prerequisite for the unavoidable resumption of the ascent.
Let the mists downhill hide for a while the distances from
view. Those mists in Steinberg's biblical phrasing hark
back to the mists of primordial creation which, in the words
of Genesis, arose and watered the earth so that the Lord
God could plant his garden in Eden, with its Tree of Life
and its Tree of Knowledge forever to challenge man's intuition to harmonize with impunity his hunger for life with
his hunger for knowledge.

Flesh of the flesh of historic Jewish experience, Palestinian literature necessarily draws much of its strength and
vitality from the idea of salvation which is so pivotal for
the entire development of the Jewish philosophy of history.
The centrality of the theme of salvation in Judaism is ex-
tremely well summarized by Martin Buber in his essay,
"The Idea of Salvation in Hasidism": "Jewish history,"
Buber observes, "manifests a distinct and distinctive phenomenon in world history. The entire historic experience
of the Jewish people centers about the one problem of exile
and redemption. The Jewish people is born out of the collective experience of the [Egyptian] exile and redemption.
In the consciousness of this people, a consciousness the like
of which is not to be found in any other human group, the
permanent bond between the past and the present bases
itself upon this initial historic event [the emergence of

Israel as a people from its exile in Egypt]. The spiritual leaders of Israel continuously declare that event of the Exodus to be a divine act in the life of Israel, the establishment of the covenant between God and his people. In the last century and a half of the First Commonwealth, in the period between the Ephraimite and Judean banishments, prophecy evolves a view of exile and redemption which remains basic for the entire development of Judaism. According to this view the very salvation of mankind, the elevation of humanity as a whole in terms of the Kingdom of God is intricately bound up with the redemption of Israel, with the elevation of Israel as the center of the hoped-for Kingdom of God. The Babylonian restoration initiates a process whereby ideas of cosmic and individual salvation—ideas stemming from oriental civilizations, particularly the Persian, and from Greece—begin to penetrate the sphere of Jewish religion, without truly blending in that period with the traditional view of the redemption of Israel. This synthesis of individual and cosmic salvation, on the one hand, and the purely Jewish element, on the other, begins only with the disintegration of the Second Commonwealth. Kabbalah especially comes to unite these alien elements, including the Gnostic conception of the redemption of the Divine Essence itself, with Jewish religion into one system whose core is Israel's hope of redemption. But the philosophy produced by this synthesis is 'the esoteric teaching,' which essentially is the possession of the few only, the possession of those initiated into the knowledge of its mysteries. In its very nature it cannot penetrate the religious life of the many, of the folk. It is only through Hasidism that the philosophy of salvation comes to dominate the psychology of ordinary man. Not merely because in Hasidism this philosophy achieves its popular formulation, but because here the individual Jew is assigned an active part in the salvation of the world."

One may question some of Buber's postulates in his brief survey of the growth of the idea of salvation in the history of Judaism. Regardless of the assumption of an earlier or later penetration into folk psychology of the various aspects of the idea of salvation, Buber's summary of the significance of this philosophy in the history of Hasidism surely applies to the bulk of traditional Jewish literature insofar as the latter stresses the role to be played by the individual Jew in the scheme of things. To the extent that the average Jew strives for self-perfection, he not only brings himself closer to personal redemption, but he also aids the group, Jewry, in its gradual advance toward redemption. And, what is equally important, by his own acts, the individual Jew enhances or vitiates the endeavors of the whole world to attain to a state of universal perfection, that state in which God himself, as it were, will have returned to his own domain. There three phases of redemption are ultimately to be achieved through Israel's return to the land God has given Israel. Jewish literature has always known the insoluble bond of people, land and God.

Modern Palestinian letters, drawing much of its sustenance from the time-honored traditional Jewish literature, shares with it the profound awareness of the sacramental quality of that triple chord of God, Israel and the land of Israel. What wonder, then, that the deepest quest in these letters is truly a quest for faith? Revaluating the longings of the Jewish past, and scanning the widening vistas of the new Jewish future, this literature cannot indeed read into the Palestinian present anything substantially different from the idea of sacredness, of continued self-perfection and self-purification which traditional literature always regarded as the bridge across which Jewry must march, over whatever turbulent gulf, toward salvation. As interpreted by this literature, the glory of Halutziut is not to be gauged by its physical achievement merely. It is rather to be measured in terms of the earnestness of purpose, of the self-dedication to the ideal which must evolve a code of *mitzvot,* of innerly prescribed and voluntarily fulfilled commandments. The performance of these *mitzvot* by the individual is at once the crystallization of his hunger for an ever more perfect state of spiritual being and his progressive contribution, day by day, and every hour of the day, to the total rehabilitation of the group, to that remarriage of land and people.

It is not surprising, therefore, to find so much of the symbolism in Palestinian writing revert to the conceptual and terminological wealth not only of traditional Jewish literature, but of traditional Jewish ritual and ceremonial as well. An ultramodernist like Abraham Shlonsky, the neo-Hebraic counterpart, in his early work, of the iconoclastic Russian Yessenin, sings of an ensuing day of physical labor in the life of the Palestinian pioneer as the dawn of another day of synagogal worship in the life of a Jewish child in Eastern Europe of days gone forever:

Clothe me, purest of mothers, in the resplendent
   coat of many colors,
And lead me to toil at dawn.
My land wraps itself in light as in the prayer shawl.
New homes stand forth as do phylacteries.
And like phylactery-bands, the highways, built by
   Jewish hands, glide.

Thus a town beautiful recites the morning prayer to
   its Creator.
Among the creators—your son Abraham,
A road-building poet in Israel.
And toward evening father will return from his labors,
And prayerfully will whisper fatherly contentment:
Sweet son, Abraham,
Mere skin and veins and bones you are—Hallelujah.

O clothe me, mother, in the resplendent coat of striped
   silk,
And, at dawn, lead me
To toil.

Uri Zevi Greenberg, so characteristically Whitmanesque in
his tendency to encase a moving lyricism in metallic cadences, reveals much the same tendency in the following
passage from his "Labor Legion," a section of his "Yeru-
shalayim shel Mattah":

And I am in the midst of the Labor Legion upon the
   shore of the Mediterranean, in the midst of
   crushing labor, which has the splendor of
   orphaned loneliness at eve. . . .

I eat my bread with them, the shewbread, and above
   them, and above me are the great steadfast stars.

All dreamed a dream like seers—and became poets who
   wrote not in a book but upon the soul.

And rhymed profound rhymes upon the tablet of the days
Until they cast their fortune like a net upon the sea,
   Until they came to the Isle of God.*

* Translated by Charles A. Cowen.

Or is there even in medieval Hebrew poetry, with the exception of Judah ha-Levi's immortal Zion elegies, anything comparable to the following outburst of love and anguished prayer for the redemption of Jerusalem, the all-inclusive symbol of Israel's historic hope of triune salvation?

> The one wall of the sanctuary you are unto me,
>   and an outpour of silence within your cliffs,
>   City and Mother, O Jerusalem!
>
> O that I would raise you up, City and Mother, beheaded
>   one, from the midst of the outpour of rocky
>   curse, like a dream and precious gift of the
>   cosmos!
>
> Then would you be always and forever, O Jerusalem, as
>   though refreshed after rain, and the moon
>   would be a healing unto you,
>
> And the olives would drip oil of myrrh upon your
>   nakedness.
>
> What shall I do for you, O City of my blood?

Palestine as the Isle of God, Jerusalem as City and Mother and Gate of Heaven, still are to the Palestinian poet what they were to his predecessors for ages and ages—the succinct meaning of the Jew's self-dedication to the vision of an ideal world, the Jew's grappling with all that is crass and ungodly in the world. The poetry of Palestine, new in form but old in many of its Jewish moods, is fed by the sacred fire of *Kiddush ha-Shem,* which is still the essence of Palestinian creativeness.

The cardinal difficulty which those unacquainted with

contemporary Palestinian life and expression encounter in their attempts to understand the fundamentally religious tone of both, lies in a relatively simple fact. Outside of Palestine, the intellectual Jew tends to confuse religiousness with the abstract formulation of creed—thinking about faith with faith itself. While the intellectual American Jew, for instance, frequently misses all the vitality of Jewish living in his endeavors to define—to himself, above all—the meaning of his Jewishness, the Palestinian Jew lives his Jewishness spontaneously, unquestioningly. Thus, with the intellectual Jew outside of Israel, theology or metaphysics becomes the be-all and end-all of his perplexities as a Jew, and almost exclusively determines for him the answer to the everlasting query: To be or not to be a Jew? In Israel, the Jew is in a more fortunate position even when perplexed by the imponderables—theological or metaphysical; he has not only the whole rich fabric of Jewish "secular" civilization to fall back upon, but also the humanism of traditional Judaism, the Jew's conviction from the time of prophecy on that the individual is the guardian of the divine expectations of man in the world and, therefore, of the world as a whole. The anthropocentricity of Judaism, its continued insistence that man, man alone, and therefore the individual Jew in particular, by his own deeds and misdeeds, shapes or mis-shapes the world, still is one of the most potent factors in Palestinian Jewish psychology. Hence, the religiousness which pervades Palestinian Hebrew letters, even while it fails to formulate its innermost beliefs, to reduce them to philosophic principles.

The imputation of religious sterility to modern Palestine, perhaps, derives from the fact that Palestine has not produced a quasi-theological or quasi-metaphysical critique of the mainsprings of its inspired living. Of course, even that is not quite true. Aside from such attempts at mystic formulation of the modern Palestinian renascence as may be found in the works of Rav Kook, similar efforts to equate the renascence with neo-orthodoxy, with traditional Judaism somewhat modernized, have been made and are constantly being made by authors who strongly lean toward a more formally religious Zionist ideology. But, what is by far more important, even the so-called "secularist" Hebrew poets and novelists—men like Shimonovitz, Fichman, Jacob Steinberg, Agnon or Kabak, experience no embarrassment in discerning the characteristically religious in the new type of Jewish self-sacrifice and self-fulfillment that they seek to capture and record in their portrayals of the new Palestine. Essentially, the true religious significance of a great part of Palestinian literary creativity is discernible in its general tendency to identify the zeal and fervor inherent in the Jewish rebirth with salvation. Those who have shouldered the brunt of bringing about Jewish redemption inspire the Palestinian poet as modern Essenes, who are at once the Gibeonites, the hewers of wood and drawers of water, and the priests and Levites in God's temple—to use a phrase of Levi ben Amittai's as he describes the end of a workday in a Kvutzah in the following stanzas:

Modest and needy is my destiny in thy world, O God!
The destiny of them that cut the wood and draw the water;
Nameless I am, one of the Gibeonites,
The eternal menials of thy Temple in Jerusalem.

And, as the sun sets, I perform the oblation—

WE HAVE traced the major trends in the development of modern Hebrew literature up to the recent truly singular events in Jewish history—the war of liberation and the establishment of the Jewish state. The impact of these events upon the cultural life of the newborn nation will prove so revolutionary as to make highly problematical any speculation concerning the ways in which the social, philosophical and artistic moods of the emergent civilization may go. At best, one may venture to suggest some of the spiritual problems being faced by the new Jewish civilization, in the light of the latest expressions of Israeli literature as compared with social aspects of the modern Hebrew literature first analyzed in this work.

We have endeavored to show that no adequate understanding of the volcanic eruption in Jewish life which led to the restoration of Israel is possible without a study of modern Hebrew letters. The continuity from the remote recesses of Jewish history to the present, linking the fate of ancient Hebrew and medieval Jew to that of the modern Jew, is tangible in the totality of the Hebrew literature of the past two hundred years. Were it not for this thread of continuity throughout the centuries, the restoration of Israel could not even have been dreamed of, let alone realized. The symbol of this spiritual thread of continuity, indeed its physical representation, has been the Hebrew language. During its long history Israel has employed and discarded many languages, in some of which very important Jewish literature has been written. But only the Hebrew language has spanned the vastness of Jewish history in time

and space. Hebrew, therefore, has proved the single reposi-
tory of Jewish existence as a whole; and its literature—including the productivity of the last two hundred years—
holds the only continuous record of Jewish vitality.

Even the most casual observer in Israel today will be im-
pressed by the heterogeneous and polyglot background of
the Jewish population. It is hardly an exaggeration to say
that every climate and civilization is represented in Israel.
But it is stating a plain fact to point out that all the Jewish
generations that have ever lived are alive today in the national consciousness of the Jews of Israel, much as the
whole of a man's past is constantly alive in his present. The
force of a common historical destiny emerging from the
Jewish past has gathered this motley multitude of occiden-
tals and orientals in the land of Israel. Granted the marvel
of Jewish history as a whole, is there any wonder that the
totality of Jewish experience now concentrated in Israel has
revived Hebrew as a vernacular?

Nor is there any wonder that of all the literatures which
have served as vehicles of expression for the modern Jew,
none has been more intimately and fatefully involved with
the resettlement of Israel's wastelands than modern Hebrew
literature. All currents of Jewish thought, every walk of
Jewish life, in all the dispersions as well as in the land of
Israel, have found their expression in modern Hebrew
literature. Indeed, the "ingathering of the exiles" that is
proceeding today in Israel is reflected in the literature by a
parallel ingathering of all Jewish cultural and spiritual
possessions. If in addition to this one considers the sensi-
tivity of the modern Hebrew writer to literary and philosophical movements in world literature, one may gain some
understanding of the inclusive diversity which has given

the Hebrew writer a sense of perspective, alongside which Jewish writing in other languages on the Jewish problem appears parochial.

We have described the premonitions which haunted modern Hebrew literature of the catastrophe that overcame European Jewry; we have dwelt on the presentiments in the literature of the messianic redemption. But above all we have stressed the fact that the conflicting moods in modern Hebrew literature were born of two ostensibly irreconcilable drives: the drive for the de-ghettoization and humanizing of Jewish life, and the equally compelling need for Jewish historic continuation. Modern Hebrew literature has participated in the broad humanistic movement that has enveloped modern Jewish life, bidding the individual Jew to leave his centuries-old ghetto. But this very process of humanization has caused the rapid disintegrating of the historic pattern of Jewish group life and has resulted in the concomitant process of assimilation, threatening the survival of the Jewish people. Out of this dilemma the perennial messianic drive to return to the land of Israel was reborn in the Zionist movement. In Zionism the conflict of the modern Jew could be resolved: the problem of Jewish continuation could be solved without sacrificing the humanistic cravings of the individual for a new and fuller life. The irresolvability of the Jewish conflict in the Diaspora made the Zionist solution a historical necessity; for while there was no returning to the ghetto, assimilation failed to give the Jew the spiritual peace and the physical security he desperately needed.

The difficulty of this conflict is nowhere recorded more sensitively than in modern Hebrew literature. No one sensed more keenly than the Hebrew writer that the Zionist

effort itself was involved in a race against time. No one
perceived more clearly that the Diaspora was rapidly disintegrating under the strain of assimilation and spiritual
decomposition within and physical extermination without.
We have seen how apprehensively Hebrew writing during
the first decades of this century views the anguished convul-
sions of the ailing modern Jew; how it fears that the Zionist
effort has come too late, perhaps, that the tide of dissolution
may prove impossible to withstand. We have also seen how
Hebrew writing finally triumphs with the emergence after
the First World War of a strong Halutz movement, with
the appearance on the scene of thousands of Jewish boys
and girls prepared to be transplanted and shoulder the task
of rebuilding the homeland. We have already analyzed the
metamorphosis which modern Hebrew literature has undergone in its discovery of Halutziut, which it has interpreted
as the process of rerooting in the ancestral soil of the historic
Jewish civilization.

Obviously, the war of liberation, 1947–48, and the subsequent establishment of the Jewish state, have confirmed
to the Hebrew author the truth of his convictions. The conflict between the humanization of Jewish life and the per-
petuation of Jewish selfhood, the perplexity underlying
Jewish existence in the modern world, as seen by the Hebrew writer, has been victoriously resolved. For the continuation of historic Jewish existence in the State of Israel
is no longer problematic. Whatever form Jewish civilization
will take in Israel, the thread of Jewish continuity will not
be broken.

Yet even in these early months of rejoicing by the literature of Israel, there are nascent sounds of a semiconscious
query which suggests that Hebrew literature is soon to be

confronted with a new problem—a problem which may
have disturbed it before the establishment of the state, but
which was kept in the background so long as the struggle
for liberation was being waged. Stated very simply the question is: What will be the balance finally struck between the
demands of Jewish tradition and those of secular humanism? To what extent will Jewish tradition color the conflu-
ence of humanism and Jewishness in Israeli civilization?
The problem presents difficulties which are uniquely Jewish. For, however complete Jewish civilization may have
been in the ghetto in every sense of the word, other than the
purely liturgical and ritualistic, it was more steeped in
the religious mood, even in its worldly aspects, than any
other, non-Jewish, civilization. Enough has been said in
this work about modern Hebrew literature also to have
suggested that, for all its humanistic aspirations, it has constantly found itself so strongly rooted in the earlier, more
purely religious moods of Jewish letters as never to have
quite severed its connections with Judaistic traditions. The
very Hebrew language in which this literature has been
produced is so charged with the quaintly synagogal that it
has been a carrier of nostalgias, however vague at times, for
the traditional past. In a deep sense Jewish history has been
the history of Judaism; and the question of the survival of
the latter in the reconstituted civilization of the Jew in his
own homeland is hardly comparable with the question of
the "separation of church and state" in modern Western
civilization.

Nor is it strictly a question of more or less religious observance in the life of the Israeli community, which is com-
posed of many observant as well as many nonobservant
Jews. The general cultural patterns of the life of the com-

munity are so imbued with Jewish tradition that even the definitely religious Jew should have little to complain of, if he bears in mind the purely religious situation in the life of any given Jewish community abroad. The daily living of Jewish folkways is a link between the Israeli present and earlier Jewish tradition. From a technical point of view, whether that of the orthodox Jew or the objective sociologist, the problem suggested may seem normal. Jewish self-rehabilitation, however, has been so powerfully impelled by complex historic yearnings that the protagonist of the new civilization to develop in Israel, the child of the dream of the perfect Jew which was envisioned by crumbling Jewish history, appears problematical precisely because, in his newness, he seems so completely different from the denizen of the ghetto who conceived him in his dream as being the perfected projection of all the ghetto-Jew was for centuries. As long as the young Palestinian product could be compacted into the messianic vision, the newness of his personality, the difference between him and his grandfather could be overlooked. Now that he has become an Israeli, the forger of a civilization in keeping with his own native propensities, the question as to his kinship with his antecedents must begin to obtrude itself more persistently. The question, also, as to his kinship with Jews in the Diaspora must become more disturbing. Hebrew literature in Israel has not yet come to formulate these questions even as consciously as some Jews visiting Israel have begun to ask them. But there can be no doubt that Israeli writers themselves will be asking them before long.

Israeli writing is already beginning to register the problem in a somewhat paradoxical way: the most popular literature in the new state is that produced by a new flock of young men, all of them "natives," all of them the hardened veterans of the war of liberation, and all of them concerned with the war and the liberation of the country as "local" patriots, whose point of departure is not at all the "messianic redemption" or the fate of the Jew outside of Israel. For instance, there is Amos Ayalon, whose novel "Jerusalem Did Not Fall" has had a sale of 12,000 copies, which certainly made it a best seller in a country with a population of 900,000. The reason the book has proved so popular is obvious. It is the story of the siege of Jerusalem by the Arabs in 1948, and it was written by an eyewitness. The success of the book is hardly accidental, for another recent novel, "In the Fields of Philistia, 1948," by Uri Abneri, has enjoyed almost equal popularity. Much the same could be said about earlier works—in fiction and in the drama—such as "In the Wastes of the Negev," by Yigal Mosenson, and "He Walked in the Fields," by Moshe Shamir.

Such self-sufficiency, centered in Israeli Jewry, may produce a literature of great vitality. But Hebrew letters, with their traditional interest in the "universal" Jew, will undoubtedly find itself confronted before long with the serious question: Where do we go from here? Can Hebrew literature in Israel—can Israeli civilization, for that matter—well afford to disengage itself from its preoccupation with the fate of the Jew and of Judaism the world over? The question has not yet been articulated, and certainly no attempt should be made to answer it here. But Hebrew literature, which has heroically resolved the dilemma of humanism versus Jewish self-continuation in modern history, may soon find itself between the horns of a new dilemma: the vision of the redemption realized in Israeli civilization versus the existence of a world Jewry not included within the scope of that vision.

PAGE

26 *Not to drive the Jew:* J. Löw Margaliot, Bet middot (Prague 1778).

27 f *In its earliest period:* Joseph Klausner, Historia shel ha-safrut ha-ivrit ha-hadashah, vol. I (Jerusalem 1920), p. 290.

31 *The crisis:* Gershom Scholem, Mitzvah ha-baa ba-averah, in Keneset, vol. II (1927), pp. 351 f.

38 *Hebrew writers:* Rabbi Menashe of Ilya, Pesher davar (1807). Judah Leib Nevohovitch, The Cry of the Daughter of Judah (Russian; 1803). Judah Hurwitz, Amude bet yehudah (1766). Isaac Satanov, Mishle Asaf (1789).

48 *We are in great distress:* M. L. Lilienblum, Collected Works (Hebrew), vol. II (1912), p. 44.

49 *Although Jews: op. cit.,* p. 53.

55 f *There are historical figures:* Ahad Haam, Al parashat dera-khim, vol. III (1921), p. 39.

57 *In their aspirations:* Joseph Klausner, Kitzur toledot ha-safrut ha-ivrit ha-hadashah, 3rd ed. (1939), pp. 82 f.

66 *The intellectuals:* Joseph Perl, Bohen zaddik (Prague 1838).

66 *Cast off:* Isaac Erter, Gilgul nefesh (1845).

76 *I consider it:* M. Kayserling, Moses Mendelssohn (1862), p. 568 (app. 57).

77 *God in his mercy: ibid.*

83 *To dedicate Jewry:* Ahad Haam, Al parashat derakhim, vol. I (1921), pp. 131 f.

84 *Our forefathers: op. cit.,* vol. II, p. 64.

84 *It is our privilege: op. cit.,* vol. II, pp. 64 f.

91 *A Jewish sadness:* Mikhah Yosef bin Gorion, Baderekh, part I (Leipzig 1922), p. 74.

92 *Man is: op. cit.,* p. 17 (text partly paraphrased).

92 *With the Haskalah:* Mikhah Yosef bin Gorion, Bisde Sefer, part I (1922), p. 133; Baderekh, part II (1922), p. 32 (text partly paraphrased).

93 *We are torn:* Mikhah Yosef bin Gorion, Baderekh, part II (1922), p. 19.

94 *We are told: op. cit.,* p. 40.

119 *To present:* Mivhar ha-sippur ha-eretz yisraeli (1938), p. 12.

167 *A strange creature:* Zevi Woislavsky, Eruve reshuyot (1944), p. 33.

186 *The God of Israel:* Yitzhak Rivkind, Elohe Bialik, in En Hakore (Berlin 1923), p. 59.

202 *Jewish history:* Martin Buber, Raayon ha-geulah ba-hasidut (Jerusalem 1942), p. 3.

GUIDE TO AUTHORS

AGNON, SHMUEL YOSEF (1888–   ) : Hebrew novelist and short story writer. He portrays the saintliness of Eastern European traditional Jewish life and its deep connection with the Land of Israel, and, at the same time, its disintegration and breakdown in the modern period. *In the Heart of the Seas* (New York 1948) relates the miracle-attended journey to the Holy Land of the pious men of Buczacz. *The Bridal Canopy* (New York 1967) presents Reb Yudel, who personifies the humble, devout, albeit naive Jew in exile, trusting in redemption. *A Guest for the Night* (New York 1968) depicts the anguish of the narrator at his belated and slowly emerging awareness that a lifelong nostalgia for his home town has dissipated. Once a seat of fervent faith and meaningful tradition, it is at present in a state of material and cultural desolation, which he records to the muted accompaniment of another, more reluctant awareness that modern Eretz-Israel is possibly the last place of refuge for Jewish spirituality. This novel, so deeply Jewish, is also universal in its development of the leitmotifs of our age: homelessness, loneliness, and alienation. Among Agnon's novellas are "Betrothed" and "Edo and Enam," which appeared together in the volume *Two Tales* (New York 1966). A treasury of traditions relating to the High Holy Days is contained in *Days of Awe* (New York 1948). The novelist was awarded the 1966 Nobel Prize for Literature.

AHAD HAAM (pseudonym for Asher Ginzberg, 1856–1927) : Most important ideologist of early Zionism. His collected essays, *Al Parashat Derakhim* ("At the Crossroads"), analyze the tendencies of the Jewish national renaissance. His philosophy molded the character of Jewish spiritual regeneration in the face of the crumbling ghetto walls when the Jew was threatened with cultural extinction. He taught that Judaism, rooted in prophetic ethics, had been an authentic force in human history and must continue. The inevitable process of modern Jewish emancipation and the tendency of Jewry to assimilate endanger the continuance of Jewish civilization. Ahad Haam therefore advocated a spiritual center in Palestine as a means for counteracting the negative forces in the Diaspora. He opposed Herzl's political Zionism with his own spiritual or cultural Zionism, maintaining that the Jewish state could not be the immediate but the final goal of the movement. To Ahad Haam, Jewish religion is a manifestation of the spirit of the people and the result, not the cause, of its urge for self-preservation. Selected essays, in English translation by Leon Simon: *Essays on Zionism and Judaism* (London 1922); *Selected Essays* (Philadelphia 1911); and *Ahad Haam: Essays, Letters, Memoirs* (Oxford 1946).

ALTERMAN, NATHAN (1910–   ): Israeli poet; he converted the Hebrew vernacular of the "man on the street" into effective poetic speech. His writings include ballads, verses on political and social events, and librettos of folk operettas.

BARASH, ASHER (1889–1952): Palestinian novelist and short story writer. His work reflects the earthiness of Galician Jewry, realistic and hearty, though containing a sense of the mystic.

BARON, DEBORAH (1887–1956): Author of portraits of ghetto characters.

BEN AMITTAI, LEVI (1901–   ): Lyrical poet of the Halutz movement.

BEN-YEHUDAH, ELIEZER (1858–1922): Author of a monumental Hebrew dictionary; he played a noteworthy part in the revival of Hebrew as a spoken language. He advocated Jewish territorial concentration in Palestine.

BERDICHEVSKY, MICAH JOSEPH (also known as Bin-Gorion, 1865–1921): Revolutionary figure in modern Hebrew literature. His work, fiction and essay, deals with the perplexed, "uprooted" Jew and the restlessness of that Jew, which stems (in B.'s characters) from the rebellion of a suppressed individualism attempting to break the shackles of the traditionalism which fettered the Jew as individual. B. advocated aestheticism and extreme secularism in Jewish life. He called for a Nietzschean transvaluation of all Jewish values, rejecting the course of Jewish history with its emphasis on the spiritual. He denounced subjugation of the people to the Book; called for the liberty to exercise man's natural passions and instincts. Paradoxically, B. himself was deeply preoccupied with Jewish spiritual history and wrote extensively on Aggadah and Hasidism.

BERKOWITZ, ISAAC DOV (1885–1967): Prose writer; translator of Sholom Aleichem's works into Hebrew. He wrote studies of Jewish folk life in White Russia, and of immigrant life in the ghettos of New York. In "Messianic Days" he presents the evolution into a Zionist of an Americanized Russian Jewish intellectual who identifies himself with the new life in the land of Israel.

BERSHADSKY, ISAIAH (pseudonym for I. Domashewitzky, 1870–1910): Novelist of the realist school; author of *Be-en Mattarah* ("Without a Goal") and *Neged ha-Zerem* ("Upstream").

BIALIK, HAYYIM NAHMAN (1873–1934): The great poet of the Hebrew renaissance. He gave expression to the sorrow of the Jew as a product of an environment of cruelty and hatred; and he depicted the Jew's despair of a world in which he is forever doomed, his pain of watching a noble ancient civilization disintegrating under the stress of homelessness. There is, therefore, no self-vaunting in B.'s nationalism. In his "Songs of Wrath" he appears as the inexorable critic of the modern Jew in conflict. B. also sings the intoxication of the modern Jew with the beauties of nature, with the longing for an ever elusive peace of mind. Yet his purely "humanistic" themes bespeak the melancholy of the selfsame modern Jew—of the individual who, in his suffering, can scarcely indulge in beauty and the joy of living. Among his major poems: *Ha-Matmid* ("The Talmud Student") ; *Be-ir ha-Haregah* ("In the City of Slaughter") ; *Mete Midbar* ("The Dead of the Wilderness") ; *Megillat ha-Esh* ("The Scroll of Fire"). B. was also an outstanding anthologist (*Sefer ha-Haggadah*), short story writer, essayist and translator from classical European literature (*Don Quixote; Wilhelm Tell*). B.'s influence on Hebrew letters and on the development of the Zionist movement is immeasurable.

BRENNER, JOSEPH HAYYIM (1881–1921) : Novelist and short story writer who dealt with the problems of the self-questioning and self-doubting Jewish intelligentsia. It was he who best, if most cruelly, presented the problem of the "uprooted," the fugitives from traditional Judaism. While his capacity for love and pity verged on the angelic, he had in his Jewish rebelliousness something of the demonic. His characters are never allowed the comfort of self-deception or the illusion of even momentary peace of mind. They are always conscious of their own failings, never tire of looking deep into their own hearts. They constantly yearn for a pure life which they are too incapacitated to achieve. Paradoxically, B.'s despair called his readers to a new creative life. He is regarded as one of the generators of the energy released in young Jewry by the pioneering in present-day Eretz Israel. His complete works were published in eight volumes. He was killed during the Arab riots of 1921.

BUBER, MARTIN (1878–1965) : Religious philosopher of world renown, spokesman for Jewish intellectual renaissance and of humanism, interpreter of the Bible. He is one of the great expounders of mysticism, in particular of Hasidism. Among his books translated into English: *I and Thou* (Edinburgh 1937), *Israel and the World* (New York

1948), *Tales of the Hasidim* (2 vols., New York 1947–48), *Eclipse of God* (New York 1952), *Pointing the Way* (New York 1957), *On Judaism* (New York 1967), *On the Bible* (New York 1968). From 1938 to 1951 he was Professor of Social Philosophy at the Hebrew University.

BURLA, JUDAH (1886–   ): Native Palestinian novelist of Sephardic origin. Exploited the rich color of the oriental milieu in numerous novels and stories dealing with the life of Bokharan, Turkish, Persian and Yemenite Jews.

CHURGIN, JACOB (1899–   ): Native Palestinian writer, author of numerous historical novels. Arab life is an important element in his stories.

COHEN, JACOB (1881–1960): Outstanding modern Hebrew poet; he reflects a harmonious integration of purely Jewish with universalistic values. Author of dramatizations of the lives of David and Solomon.

EBER HADANI (1899–   ): Palestinian novelist. His work expresses the pathos of the pioneers' struggle in Palestine.

ERTER, ISAAC (1792–1851): Haskalah satirist. Wrote *Hatzofeh le-Vet Yisrael* ("Watchman of the House of Israel"), sketches of Galician folk Hasidism picturing the moral defections which appeared under the guise of ghetto religiosity.

EUCHEL, ISAAC (1756–1804): One of the earliest of the Haskalah writers. He was an editor and contributor of *Measef,* first modern Hebrew periodical of the enlightenment movement. E. maintained that Haskalah was not incompatible with authentic religious belief. He wrote a biography of Moses Mendelssohn.

FICHMAN, JACOB (1881–1958): Poet, essayist, critic and anthologist, living in Palestine since 1912. In his literary criticism he has come to be increasingly preoccupied with the creators of modern Hebrew letters.

FREIMAN, ABRAHAM (1886– d.?): Russian-born Hebrew writer. Wrote the two-volume novel, "1919," dealing with Jewish life in pogrom-ridden Ukraine during the Bolshevik Revolution.

GOLDBERG, LEAH (1911–   ): Lithuanian-born Palestinian poetess and critic. Her nature poems are drawn from the scenes of her childhood.

GORDON, AARON DAVID (1850–1922): Philosopher of the Halutz movement. He formulated the so-called "religion of labor" doctrine which became the ideological basis for the self-consecration to creative physical labor of the pioneering movement in Palestine.

GORDON, JUDAH LEIB (1830–1892): Leading Haskalah poet, advocate of social, communal, educational and religious reforms. In his romantic early period, G. wrote historical idylls on the advantages of rustic life; he was taken in by the passing wave of liberalism of the reign of Alexander II. In his realistic middle period, G. attacked rabbinic Judaism in satirical verse caricaturing the evil effects of outmoded Jewish laws. After the pogroms of 1881–82, he lost faith in enlightenment as a panacea for the Jewish problem; a pessimistic, nihilistic mood pervades his poetry of the period.

GROSSMAN, REUBEN (1905–   ): American-born Palestinian poet, influenced by the Anglo-American poetic tradition.

GREENBERG, URI ZEVI (1894–   ): Palestinian poet, concentrating in his poetry on the establishment of a sovereign Hebrew nation in Zion. Has written some of the most poignant religious poetry in modern Hebrew literature, and powerful elegies over the destruction of European Jewry. His *Sefer ha-Kitrug ve-ha-Emunah* ("Book of Accusation and Belief"), 1937, expresses his political and poetic viewpoint.

HAMEIRI, AVIGDOR (1890–   ): Palestinian poet, novelist

and short story writer. His "The Great Madness" reflects the throes of the Jewish redemption.

HAZAZ, HAYYIM (1898–): Ukrainian-born Palestinian novelist and short story writer. Presents the life of Jewry in European capitals during the period of crucial change which uprooted the foundations of Jewish existence. His work includes short stories on the biblical period and a novel dealing with Yemenite Jews in Palestine.

HURWITZ, SAUL ISRAEL (1860–1922): Hebrew thinker and scholar. In his *Meayyin Ulean* ("Whence and Whither") he questioned the historic continuation of the Jewish people.

IMBER, NAPHTALI HERZ (1856–1931): Author of *Hatikvah;* one of the first modern settlers in Palestine, he published in 1886 a collection of poems in which he celebrated the newly established colonies.

JAWITZ, ZEEV WOLF (1848–1924): Hebrew historian, writer of fiction and essayist. His *Sefer Toledot Yisrael*, thirteen volumes, is an account of Jewish history in the spirit of orthodox Judaism.

KABAK, ABRAHAM ABBA (1883–1944): Novelist. In his two-volume novel, *Bamishol Hatzar* ("On the Narrow Path"), K. makes Jesus of Nazareth the central figure. K.'s trilogy presents the metamorphosis of the 16th century Marrano Jew, Solomon Molcho, into the martyred visionary. His final, unfinished work is a saga tracing the story of a Jewish family in the course of the last one hundred years.

KARNI, JUDAH (1884–1949): Poet of the Palestinian landscape and of the Jew who is rooting himself in that landscape.

KLAUSNER, JOSEPH (1874–1958): Professor for a period of years of modern Hebrew literature at the Hebrew University in Jerusalem; influential modern Hebrew thinker, literary critic, historian and publicist. For him, Judaism and humanism are co-extensive and tantamount values. Wrote a history of modern Hebrew literature and a history of the Jews in the Second Commonwealth. Available in English: *A History of Modern Hebrew Literature* (London 1932); *Jesus of Nazareth* (New York 1925); *From Jesus to Paul* (New York 1943).

HA-KOHEN, SHALOM (1772–1845): Haskalah writer who revived *Measef* in 1809. After the renaissance of modern Hebrew literature had petered out in Germany, he was instrumental in transferring it to Eastern Europe. Established *Bikkure ha-Ittim,* Hebrew literary annual issued for twelve years.

KROCHMAL, NAHMAN (1785–1840): Original Jewish thinker of the Haskalah period. His *Moreh Nebukhe ha-Zeman* ("Guide to the Perplexed of the Age") was published posthumously (1851) by Zunz; it is a system of philosophy of Judaism as an organic national civilization. K. is one of the founders of "science of Judaism." His studies blazed the path for subsequent generations of students of Bible, Talmud, rabbinics and Jewish philosophy and mysticism.

LAMDAN, YITZHAK (1900–1954): Palestinian poet. His *Masada* (last Jewish fortress held against the Romans) portrays the Halutz movement as the last-ditch fight of modern Jewry for national survival. Another work revives the figure of Rabbi Akiba, saintly leader during the Bar Kokhba revolt.

LEBENSOHN, MICAH JOSEPH (known as Michal; 1828–1852): Son of the Haskalah poet Abraham Dob Lebensohn. Imaginative, sensitive Hebrew poet. Wrote *Shire Bat Zion* ("Songs of the Daughter of Zion") and *Kinor Bat Zion* ("The Harp of the Daughter of Zion").

LEVIN, SHEMARYA (1867–1935): Zionist leader and thinker; outstanding public speaker. His autobiography and memoirs picture Jewish life in Russia during the past several generations.

LEVINSOHN, ISAAC BAER (1788–1860): Author of *Teudah be-Yisrael* ("A Testimony in Israel") and *Bet Yehudah* ("The House of Judah"), which were instrumental in disseminating Haskalah among Russian Jews.

LEVISOHN, SOLOMON (1789–1822): Haskalah poet, historian and linguist. His *Mehkere Aretz* ("Studies in the Geography of the Holy Land") is the first geographical and historical dictionary of the Bible.

LILIENBLUM, MOSHE LEIB (1843–1910): Publicist; pressed for socio-economic and cultural reform in Jewish life, and for relaxing unduly stringent religious observance. After the pogroms of 1881 he was convinced that the Jews were everywhere aliens and their problems irresolvable in the Diaspora. He became a leading protagonist of the Hibbat Zion movement.

LUZZATTO, EPHRAIM (1729–1792): Italian-born Hebrew writer of the Haskalah. Wrote songs of friendship, elegies, satires, lyrics, religious poems and love poems.

LUZZATTO, MOSES HAYYIM (1707–1747): Italian-born Hebrew mystic and poet, called the "father of modern Hebrew literature." His poetry was strongly humanistic: chiefly pastoral dramas or dramatic allegories celebrating the beauties of nature, love and friendship, and the sense of metaphysical wonder roused by contemplation of the universe. His mystical activities were a source of friction between him and the Jewish community. He made a pilgrimage to Palestine, in order, perhaps, to realize there the dream of his youth: through occult kabbalistic forces, to gather the scattered remnants of Jewry in its homeland. But his life was cut short by the plague at Akko. The fascinating figure of Luzzatto straddles the Middle Ages and modern times. He lived in the psychological world of the medieval Jew, yet he assimilated into this world the aesthetic and formal values of the secular Italian and classical literature of his day. Luzzatto's masterful use of Hebrew revitalized the language which over the centuries had grown sterile in conventionally rigid literary forms. His allegorical dramas revitalized Hebrew poetry.

LUZZATTO, SAMUEL DAVID (1800–1865): Scholar of encyclopedic knowledge. He rigorously upheld the orthodox standpoint in Judaism, though he allowed himself to suggest emendations in the text of the Bible. L. maintained that Judaism and Hellenism are two irreconcilably opposite poles of human existence. He was critical of Maimonides for attempting their reconciliation. The nationalist philosophy of Jewish history he developed presaged the Hebrew national renaissance.

MAIMON, SOLOMON (1754–1800): Philosopher of brilliant intellect; eccentric in character. He translated scientific books into Hebrew, and, in his later years, produced philosophical writings. Best known for his *Autobiography* (Schocken Library No. 5).

MALETZ, DAVID (1900–   ): Israeli novelist and short story writer, mainly concerned with problems of Kvutzah life. His *Maagalot* appeared in English as *Young Hearts* (New York 1950).

MAPU, ABRAHAM (1808–1868): First modern Hebrew novelist. His most popular works were romances based upon the biblical history of the Northern Kingdom. His portrayal of rustic Jewish life in the sovereign state of ancient Israel stirred the imagination of his readers and made them long for a return to those glorious times. His novels, therefore, were a factor in the development of the Zionist movement. His *Ayit Tzavua* ("The Painted Vulture") is a satirical analysis of Jewish obscurantism among 19th century Lithuanian Jewry.

MAZEH, JACOB (1860–1924): Zionist leader, and rabbi in Moscow. His memoirs picture Jewish life in Russia.

MENDELE MOCHER SEFORIM (pseudonym for Shalom Jacob Abramowitz, 1836–1918): Important Hebrew novelist of traditional East European Jewish life of the mid-19th century. M. has been called the "grandfather" (*sava*) of Hebrew (and Yiddish) literature. He satirized all that was unwholesome and sterile in the ghetto of Eastern Europe. His novels, first written in Yiddish and later rewritten in Hebrew, are a museum of Jewish realia. His style, which made use of mishnaic and midrashic idiom, played a decisive role in the development of modern Hebrew writings. His novelette *The Travels of Benjamin the Third* is available in English translation (Schocken Library No. 18).

MENDELSSOHN, MOSES (1729–1786): Haskalah period's "second Moses." With the emergence of the Jewish national renaissance, Mendelssohn's reputation was seriously tarnished. He edited the short-lived Hebrew periodical *Kohelet Musar* (1750). Wrote "Jerusalem," outlining religious and political toleration, separation of church and state, and equality for all citizens. Edited a German translation of the Bible with a Hebrew commentary (*Biur*) which helped to spread enlightenment.

PERETZ, ISAAC LEIB (1851–1915): Master of the short story in Yiddish and Hebrew. Noted for his revaluation and idealization of Hasidism in the early days of the Jewish national renaissance. His work is saturated with the symbolism of Jewish folk life; his aestheticized version of Jewish religion and mysticism was very influential.

PINES, YEHIEL MICHEL (1843–1913): Spokesman of the Hibbat Zion movement. His *Yalde Ruhi* ("Children of My Spirit"), published in 1872, interpreted Jewish tradition and ritual as the poetic expression of the intellectual and emotional life of Israel.

RABINOWITZ, ALEXANDER SISKIND (1854–1946): Hebrew story writer, publicist and pedagogue; he was one of the earliest leaders of the Hibbat Zion movement.

RABINOV, JOSHUA (1905–   ): Palestinian Hebrew poet who describes the Palestinian landscape and life on a Kvutzah.

RACHEL (Bluwstein; 1890–1931): Palestinian lyrical poetess. The landscape of the Jordan valley and the Sea of Galilee, the everyday life of a Halutz, the experience of taking root in the biblical homeland, are some of the motifs of her poetry.

RIMMON, JOSEPH ZEVI (1889–1958): Polish-born Hebrew poet, intense and ecstatic in mood; drive for messianic redemption is a leitmotif in his work.

SATANOV, ISAAC (1732–1805): Haskalah thinker and follower of Mendelssohn. Published commentaries to Maimonides' *Guide to the Perplexed,* and Judah ha-Levi's *Kuzari.* Author of *Mishle Asaf* ("Parables of Asaph").

SCHOFMANN, GERSHOM (1880–   ): Short story writer; portrays the self-searching, maladjusted Jewish intellectual. His writings appeared in four volumes (Tel Aviv 1927–1931). Also, Schofmann has translated into the Hebrew short pieces by Peter Altenberg, by whom he was influenced.

SECO, MEIR (pseudonym for Meir Smilanski, 1876–   ):
Ukrainian-born Palestinian story writer, portrayer of hasidic
life in the Ukraine, and the horrors of the pogroms of 1919–
1921.

SHALOM, SH. (pseudonym for Shalom Shapiro, 1905–   ):
Palestinian poet, concerned with the personal and national redemption of the contemporary Jew. S. was born in Poland of
an aristocratic hasidic family; his poetry bespeaks his kabbalistic heritage.

SHENBERG, YITZHAK (1905–1957): Short story writer belonging to the younger group of Israeli writers. Highly gifted, he
portrays modern Jews and Jewesses hailing from different
parts of Central and Eastern Europe; he communicates the
emotional trials of the new Jewish settler who has not yet
completed the process of spiritual transplantation from his
old home. Shenberg excels in his polished, cultivated style
and the restraint with which he employs his colorful Hebrew
idiom. English selection of his stories: *Under the Fig Tree*
(Schocken Library No. 13).

SHIMONOVITZ, DAVID (1886–1959): Popular Palestinian poet.
His "idylls" are dramatic poems of the pain and the bliss
which the Jewish pioneer has experienced in his contact with
the land of Israel. S. realizes that in the land of Israel the Jew
has begun to reshape himself individually while building the
Jewish future.

SHLONSKY, ABRAHAM (1900–   ): Palestinian poet. His
poetry mirrors, on the one hand, the chaotic state of a world
which has inflicted pogroms on the Jew; and on the other, the
struggles of the Halutz consecrated to creative toil. Much of
his poetry has been put to music.

SHNEUR, ZALMAN (1886–1959): Eminent Hebrew poet and
prose writer. He is defiant of tradition, almost blasphemous in

questioning the accepted standards of religion, morality and the eternal verities. Mechanical civilization seems to him to be the cause of the degeneration of man. Yet this almost Nietzschean iconoclast is deeply Jewish in his attempt to identify the petrifaction of human life with an idolatry which was fought by the spirit of Israel. S. calls his people to remain true to itself, so that once again it may become the protagonist of spiritual values in the drama of history. His novel *Noah Pandre* appeared also in English (1936).

SHOHAM, MATTATHIAH (1898–1938): Writer of poetical dramas which are modernist studies of biblical history. Author also of lyric poetry and short philosophical essays.

SHOLOM ALEICHEM (pseudonym for Sholem Rabinowitz, 1859–1916): One of the "fathers" of modern Yiddish literature, along with Mendele and Peretz. He began writing in Hebrew but soon turned to Yiddish. In that language he became the greatest Jewish humorist. English rendition of his Kasrilevke stories: *Inside Kasrilevke* (Schocken Library No. 11).

SHULMAN, KALMAN (1819–1899): Haskalah writer. Produced the popular compendiums, *Divre Yeme Olam* ("A History of the World") and *Divre Yeme Hayehudim* ("A History of the Jews").

SMOLENSKIN, PERETZ (1842–1885): Novelist. As early as the 1870's he published *Am Olam* ("An Eternal People") and *Et Lataat* ("Time to Plant"), demanding nationalism as opposed to cosmopolitanism. Active spokesman of the Hibbat Zion movement.

STEINBERG, JACOB (1886–1947): Individualist poet and essayist who recorded the involutions of his intellectual and emotional life. Settled in Palestine in the early years of the pioneering period. In his lyrics and especially in his essays, he glorified the eternal covenant between Israel and its land. Early a skeptic and pessimist, he became a poet of faith verging on saintliness. Author also of stories on the life of Jewish farmers in the Ukraine.

STEINBERG, JUDAH (1863–1908): Short story writer who portrayed hasidic life.

TCHERNICHOVSKY, SAUL (1875–1943): Great modern Hebrew poet. Outwardly, his poetry appears to be Hebraic only in idiom; in subject matter it is largely universal. In almost pagan terms, he worships the might and beauty of creative cosmic nature and celebrates the gods of the ancient and classical worlds. His love lyrics never betray a sense of Jewish asceticism or otherworldliness. Yet, for all his ingrained universalism and humanism, T. also proved the poet of the historic Jewish tragedy as well as the singer of the most fervent faith in Jewish survival. In his ballads based upon Jewish martyrology of the Middle Ages (e.g., "Baruch of Mayence"), he depicted the cruelty perpetrated upon the Jew by his environment, as well as the Jewish resentment of that environment. He portrayed the simplicity and endurance of Jewish folk life in his "idylls." In his Palestinian period he identified himself with Jewish national rebirth (e.g., *Rei Adamah,* "See Here, Earth"). T. translated the Iliad, the Odyssey, the Finnish epic *Kalevala,* Longfellow's *Hiawatha,* Plato's *Symposium,* Goethe's poems, Anacreon's songs and the works of Horace.

WESSELY, NAFTALI HERZ (1725–1805): Hebrew poet and Jewish educator; brought up in Copenhagen. He wrote a philological work on Hebrew synonyms. W. became acquainted with Mendelssohn and championed the enlightenment, contributing the Hebrew commentary on Leviticus for Mendelssohn's Pentateuch. W. wrote *Divre Shalom ve-Emet* ("Words of Peace and Truth"), urging the Jews of Austria to accept the Tolerance Edict of Emperor Joseph II. His *Shire Tiferet* ("Mosaide"), in five parts, modeled on Klopstock's "Messiade," poeticizes the figure of Moses and the story of the Exodus, and discourses on the virtues of the soul in its aspirations toward the sublime. It was the first successful attempt to use Hebrew in modern European manner.

YAARI, JUDAH (1900–   ): Palestinian fiction writer; presented human side of Halutziut and frequently tended toward a mystical interpretation of it.

ZEITLIN, HILLEL (1872–1943): Popular Hebrew and Yiddish writer of a semiphilosophical and semimystical bent. He was killed in the annihilation of the Warsaw ghetto.